Philip Gilbert Hamerton

Chapters on Animals

Philip Gilbert Hamerton

Chapters on Animals

ISBN/EAN: 9783337240622

Printed in Europe, USA, Canada, Australia, Japan

Cover: Foto ©Andreas Hilbeck / pixelio.de

More available books at **www.hansebooks.com**

Chapters on Animals.

BY

PHILIP GILBERT HAMERTON,

AUTHOR OF "THE INTELLECTUAL LIFE," "A PAINTER'S CAMP," "THOUGHTS
ABOUT ART," "THE UNKNOWN RIVER," ETC.

BOSTON:
ROBERTS BROTHERS.
1882.

UNIVERSITY PRESS: JOHN WILSON & SON,
CAMBRIDGE.

PREFACE.

HAVING been in the habit of loving and observing animals, as people do who live much in the country, I thought that possibly some of my observations, however trifling in themselves, might interest others whose tastes are similar to my own. In this spirit I wrote these chapters, describing what I had seen rather than what other writers had recorded. The book has therefore no pretension to system or completeness, but consists merely of desultory chapters, as its title indicates.

P. G. H.

CONTENTS.

CHAPTER.		PAGE.
I.	THE LIFE OF THE BRUTE	1
II.	DOGS	17
III.	DOGS (continued)	32
IV.	CATS	43
IV*.	HORSES	61
V.	HORSES (continued)	77
VI.	THE BOVINES	96
VII.	ASSES	113
VIII.	PIGS	127
IX.	WILD BOARS	142
X.	WOLVES	156
XI.	KIDS	174
XII.	OTHER ANIMALS	188
XIII.	BIRDS	197
XIV.	BIRDS (continued)	207
XV.	ANIMALS IN ART	221
XVI.	CANINE GUESTS	236

CHAPTERS ON ANIMALS.

CHAPTER I.

THE LIFE OF THE BRUTE.

READERS of Dean Stanley's *Life of Dr. Arnold* will probably remember a passage, brief but highly interesting, in which reference is made to his feelings about the brute creation;—'In works of art he took but little interest, and any extended researches in physical science were precluded by want of time, whilst from natural history he had an instinctive but characteristic shrinking. "The whole subject," he said, "of the brute creation is to me one of such painful mystery, that I dare not approach it."'

Mystery indeed there is everywhere, and it is often painful; but surely in shrinking from the contemplation of nature the loss is greater than the gain. That all animals are condemned at one period or another of their existence to undergo suffering, often very severe suffering, and that in their utmost anguish they have no consolation from religious or philosophical ideas, that they have no hope beyond the limits of a day, and that their existence is most probably limited to the brief space between birth and death,—this is the dark side of their being, which we need not attempt to hide. But, on the other hand, the life of the brute has commonly one immense compensation in its favour, the perfection of the individual existence is so rarely sacrificed to the prosperity of the race. It is not necessary in order that one hippopotamus should cut his food conveniently that another hippopotamus should lead an unhealthy existence like a Sheffield grinder; nor does the comfort of any bird's nest require that another bird should slowly poison itself in preparing acetates of copper, sulphurets of mercury, or oxides of lead. The pride and beauty of a brute are never based upon the enduring misery of another brute. The wild drake's plumage, splendid as it is, suggests no painful thought of consumptive weavers, of ill-paid lace-makers, of harassed, over-worked milliners; and the most sensitive of us may enjoy the sight of it without painful thoughts, for it is God's free gift, causing no heart-burning of envy, no care nor anxiety of any kind. There is much slaughter in the world of brutes, but there is little slavery, and the killing is done with a merciful rapidity, ending life whilst its pulses still beat in their energy, and preventing infirmity and age. The brute creation has its diseases, but on the whole it is astonishingly healthy. It is full of an amazing vitality.* The more we study animals the more evident is it that they live for the most part in the heaven of exuberant health. That gladness which we seek, how often vainly, in all artificial stimulants,—in wine, tea, gin, tobacco, opium, and the rest,—the brute finds in the free coursing of his own uncontaminated blood. Our nervous miseries, our brain-exhaustion, are unknown to him. Has not one of the sweetest of our poets, who knew those miseries of the intellectual, poured forth in immortal verse his passionate longing for the 'clear keen joyance' of a skylark? Which of us has not envied the glee of his own dog? Human happiness may be deeper, but it is never, after earliest infancy, so free from all shadow of sadness or regret.

It is probable that Dr. Arnold's disinclination for the study of animal life, and his painful feelings regarding it, had their origin in a peculiarity of his which made him such an excellent schoolmaster—the intense pleasure with which he contemplated moral and intellectual advance, a pleasure which had for its shadow a feeling of intense disgust for incorrigibles. To a man with these feelings always highly-wrought, and even rather over-excited by the nature of his work, a man always anxious to make good Christians and cultivated gentlemen, the brute world must have seemed a very discouraging kind of material.

* This in consequence of the law, apparently pitiless, yet when seen in its large results most merciful, that the weak and diseased so rapidly die off, that the strong and healthy remain and propagate, whilst the organizations ill adapted for vigourous life perish and disappear.

What changes nature may operate in millions of years, what marvellous developments may lead up gradually to higher orders of being, we need not attempt to estimate; it is enough for us, that from the dawn of history the animals most familiarly known to us seem to have done the same things, and done them in the same way, as their successors in our own fields and on our own hearth-rugs. We have evidence that the donkeys of antiquity were obstinate and self-willed, and the donkeys of the nineteenth century are so still. But in this persistence of characteristics there is nothing, I think, to sadden us. The brute does not, it is true, aspire after the ideal, and his views, it must be confessed, are usually limited to the fullest and most immediate gratification of his appetites, but he has so many negative advantages that we may think and speak of him with cheerfulness. If he has not the support and consolations of religion it is because he does not require them, and he escapes the evils of theological rancour and persecution which have caused so much misery to mankind. He escapes, too, the meanness of hypocrisy, which is one of the least pleasing of the peculiarly human vices. So with regard to the politics of brutes—they are royalists, or republicans, or socialists, or they push to an extreme impossible for mankind the principles of independent individualism; but whatever they are they know their own mind, and incur neither the evils of anarchy nor the perils of transition. How much weariness has there been in the human race during the last fifty years, because the human race cannot stop politically where it was, and, finding no rest, is pushed to a strange future that the wisest look forward to gravely, as certainly very dark and probably very dangerous! Meanwhile have the bees suffered any political uneasiness, have they doubted the use of royalty or begrudged the cost of their Queen? Have those industrious republicans, the ants, gone about uneasily seeking after a sovereign? Has the eagle grown weary of his isolation and sought strength in the practice of socialism? Has the dog become too enlightened to endure any longer his position as man's humble friend, and contemplated a canine union for mutual protection against masters? No, the great principles of these existences are superior to change, and that which man is perpetually seeking, a political order in perfect harmony with his condition, the brute has inherited with his instincts.

The study of animals inclines men to a steady cheerfulness. All naturalists are cheerful men, unless there is something peculiarly sad or painful in the individual lot; and even then the study of natural history has in many instances been known to supply an interest which enabled the sufferer to bear his affliction more easily. The contemplation of animal life may act at once as a stimulant and an anodyne. The abounding vitality of animals communicates a strong stimulus to those energies which we have in common with them, whilst on the other hand their absolute incapacity for sharing our higher intellectual vitality has a tendency to make us happily forget it in their presence. Your dog will run and jump with you as much as you like, but it is of no use to talk to him about your business anxieties or your literary ambition. I believe that most of the attractiveness of what is called 'sport,' is to be found in the happiness of association with the lower animals. Take away the animals from a hunt; suppose that there were neither horses nor dogs, nor stag, fox, wild boar, or any other animal whatever, but that the men rode on velocipedes after a machine going by electricity—who does not at once feel that the deep charm of the chase would be gone? Few will deny that falconry, though far less destructive than shooting, was a more perfect sport; for the falconer associated himself with the bird of prey that he had trained with hood and jesses and lure, and watched its aerial evolutions. The pleasure of falconry was to be a spectator at one's own hours of a sight which every naturalist has occasionally witnessed in his rambles—the bird of prey in the exercise of his terrible function. The noble of the middle ages, who was a bird of prey himself by instinct and tradition, felt the deepest sympathy with the hawk, and carried him everywhere on his wrist as poor women carry their babies; but the modern student of nature may sympathise with the hawk also, notwithstanding our modern tenderness. We may always sympathise with an animal, because the animal is sure to do his appointed work; the business of the falcon being to destroy birds for his own sustenance, he does it without any infirmity of doubt. He hurls himself like a barbed javelin, and the sharp talon delivers its deadly stroke. Since the work, in Nature's order, had to be done, there is a satisfaction in seeing it done with that swiftness and decision, that perfect vigour and ability. So the old knights often took the falcon for a crest, and he sat in effigy on their helmets, tossed above the dust of the battle-field.

But the knight's sympathy or the sportsman's sympathy for animals is more narrow, though not more intense by reason of its narrowness, than the sympathy of the naturalist or artist. Since falconry is dead the falcon would be doomed to extinction if gamekeepers had their way; and the sportsman thinks that if an animal is not either good to hunt or be hunted, does not play the part either of hound or hare, there can be no sufficient reason against its total extermination. So the agriculturist has *his* way of considering animals, with *his* two categories— the beasts that can work for him and the beasts that can be sold to the butcher. But there is another way besides these, that of the observer who studies the aninal from some kind of interest in nature without reference to anything that it can do for him or produce for him. The selfish pre-occupation always hinders us from observing in the best and largest sense. Some excellent observers have been sportsmen and agriculturists; this partly from accident, because they had land in the country, and partly from hereditary tendencies derived from sporting or agricultural ancestors: but it is possible to kill animals every day, and make animals work all day long, and sell animals at every fair in the neighbourhood, without knowing very much more about their lives and characters than they know of yours and mine. I have seen men who had not the least insight into the characters of their own horses or their own dogs. It grates very unpleasantly on the feelings of any true lover of animals to see them treated as beings without any individuality of mental constitution. There are people to whom a horse is a horse, just as a penny postage-stamp is a penny postage-stamp; that is, a thing which will convey a certain weight for a certain regulated distance. But any one who knows animals knows that a horse has as much individuality as a man. And the more we know, even of inferior animals, the more distinct does their individuality become for us. It is only our ignorance and our indifference which confound them. The two bay horses in your carriage look exactly alike to the people in the street, but the coachman and groom could establish contrasts and comparisons after the manner of Plutarch. With the varieties of canine character we are all of us tolerably familiar, because our dogs are more with us, happily for us and for them. Yet how difficult it is to arrive at any *true* conception of the mind of a lower animal! The moment we begin to reason about it a thick cloud rises and comes between. We speak of them habitually as if they had human feelings: a dog is spoken of very much as if he were a child, yet he is not a child; and we give to horses many capacities and attributes which horses never possess. There is an insuperable difficulty in imagining the mind of an animal; we lend him words, which he never uses, to express thoughts which could not occur to him. We are constantly misled by the evident clearness of the minds of animals, by the acuteness of their perceptions in certain directions, and we infer that this clearness and acuteness may be applied where they are of no use. The truth is, that animals are both more intelligent and less intelligent than we fancy. A dog, and even a horse, notices a good deal that we little suspect him of noticing, but at the same time a great deal which we think he sees is perfectly invisible to him. The following account of the behaviour of a cow gives a glimpse of the real nature of the animal:—

'These long-tailed cows,' say Messrs. Huc and Gabet, 'are so restive and difficult to milk, that, to keep them at all quiet, the herdsman has to give them a calf to lick meanwhile. But for this device, not a single drop of milk could be obtained from them. One day a Lama herdsman, who lived in the same house with ourselves, came, with a long dismal face, to announce that his cow had calved during the night, and that, unfortunately, the calf was dying. It died in the course of the day. The Lama forthwith skinned the poor beast, and stuffed it with hay. This proceeding surprised us at first, for the Lama had by no means the air of a man likely to give himself the luxury of a cabinet of natural history. When the operation was completed we found that the hay-calf had neither feet nor head; whereupon it occurred to us that, after all, it was perhaps a pillow that the Lama contemplated. We were in error; but the error was not dissipated till the next morning, when our herdsman went to milk his cow. Seeing him issue forth, the pail in one hand

and the hay-calf under the other arm, the fancy occurred to us to follow him. His first proceeding was to put the hay-calf down before the cow. He then turned to milk the cow herself. The mamma at first opened enormous eyes at her beloved infant; by degrees she stooped her head towards it, then smelt at it, sneezed three or four times, and at last proceeded to lick it with the most delightful tenderness. This spectacle grated against our sensibilities; it seemed to us that he who first invented this parody upon one of the most touching incidents in nature must have been a man without a heart. A somewhat burlesque circumstance occurred one day to modify the indignation with which this treachery inspired us. By dint of caressing and licking her little calf, the tender parent one fine morning unripped it; the hay issued from within, and the cow, manifesting not the slightest surprise nor agitation, proceeded tranquilly to devour the unexpected provender.'

The last touch entirely paints the brute. She has recognised her offspring by the smell chiefly, and never having heard of anatomy is not surprised when the internal organs are found to consist simply of hay. And why not eat the hay? The absence of surprise at the discovery, the immediateness of the decision to eat the hay, are perfectly natural in a cow, and if they surprise us it is only because we do not fully realise the state of the bovine mind. If we reflect, however, we must perceive that a cow can be aware of no reason why calves should not be constructed internally of hay. On the other hand, the bovine mind cannot be wanting in its own kind of intelligence, for oxen know their masters, and when in harness are remarkable for a very accurate and delicate kind of obedience; indeed the horse is light-headed and careless in comparison with them.

Animals, like the great majority of the human race, observe only what concerns them and see everything simply in the relation which it bears to themselves. In Gustave Doré's 'Juif Errant' a donkey is tasting a man's beard, under the impression that it may possibly be a sort of hay. Doré most probably had witnessed the incident; I have witnessed it several times. Why should a man's beard not consist of hay? There are physiological reasons, but we cannot expect a donkey to be aware of them. We continually forget that brutes have not the advantage of obtaining accurate ideas by spoken or written language. We do not realise the immensity of their ignorance. That ignorance, in combination with perfect cerebral clearness (ignorance and mental clearness are quite compatible), and with inconceivable strong instincts, produces a creature whose mental states we can never accurately understand. None of us can imagine the feelings of a tiger when his jaws are bathed in blood and he tears the quivering flesh. The passion of the great flesh-eater is as completely unknown to civilised men, as the passion of the poet is to the tiger in the jungle. It is far more than merely a good appetite, it is an intense emotion. A quite faint and pale shadow of it still remains in men with an ardent enthusiasm for the chase, who feel a joy in slaughter, but this to the tiger's passion is as water to whisky. This impossibility of knowing the real sensations of animals—and the sensations are the life—stands like an inaccessible and immovable rock right in the pathway of our studies. The effort of dramatic power necessary to imagine the life of another person is very considerable, and few minds are capable of it, but it is much easier to imagine the sensations of a farmer than those of his horse. The main difficulty in conceiving the mental states of animals is, that the moment we think of them as *human* we are lost. Neither are they machines pushed by irresistible instincts. A human being as ignorant as a horse would be an idiot, and act with an idiot's lack of sense and incapacity for sequence. But the horse is not an idiot, he has a mind at once quite clear and sane, and is very observant in his own way. Most domestic animals are as keenly alive to their own interests as a man of business. They can make bargains, and stick to them, and make you stick to them also. I have a little mare who used to require six men to catch her in the pasture, but I carried corn to her for a long time without trying to take her, leaving the corn on the ground. Next, I induced her to eat the corn whilst I held it, still leaving her free. Finally I persuaded her to follow me, and now she will come trotting half-a-mile at my whistle, leaping ditches, fording brooks, in the darkness and rain, or in impenetrable fog. She follows me like a dog to the stable, and I administer the corn there. But it is a bargain; she knowingly sells her liberty for the corn. The experiment of reducing the reward having been tried to test her behaviour, she ceased to obey the whistle and resumed her former habits; but the full and due quantity having been restored she yielded her liberty again without resistance, and since then she is not to be cheated. On the other hand, she is very ignorant of much that a man of equal shrewdness would easily have picked up by the use of language. In our estimates of animal character we always commit one of two mistakes,—either we conclude that the beasts have great knowledge because they seem so clever, or else we fancy that they must be stupid because we have ascertained that they are ignorant; so that, on the one hand, we constantly see animals severely punished for not having known what they could only have learned through human language, and, on the other hand, we find men very frequently underrating the wonderful natural intelligence of the brute creation, and treating animals without the least consideration for their feelings, which are often highly sensitive.

Another obstacle to a right understanding of the brute nature is the common habit of sentimentalism, which attributes to some favourite races of animals some fine qualities, which, if they are to be discovered at all, can only be detected in most rare instances, and, even then, are striking rather from their rarity than their strength. A good example of what I mean is the popular belief concerning the affectionateness of horses. The plain truth is, that the horse is not an affectionate animal but that man wishes he were so, and supplies him with this charming quality from the resources of his own imagination. The horse may be made familiar; you may cultivate his intimate acquaintance, as acquaintance merely, but his affections are not for man, they are for his brute companions.*

It seems to me, that notwithstanding the insuperable difficulties which hinder us from a perfect comprehension of the brute nature in any of its forms, we may still, by careful observation and reflection, aided by a kindly sympathy and indulgence, arrive at notions about animal life not altogether without interest. Let us always try to bear in mind those great necessities which are irresistibly felt by animals as a consequence of their special organisation, and preserve ourselves from the error of approving or blaming them according to human standards. When a tiger eats a man, the act is not more blameable than the act of a man who opens and eats an oyster We have the most absurd prejudices on this subject, which have taken root in infancy and not been disturbed by maturer reflection afterwards. Wolves and falcons seem cruel because their prey is rather large, but the little insect-eating birds are our pets, and cats are morally esteemed for catching mice. A word may be said in passing about the morbid love which many people have for animals, and foolishly encourage as a virtue. Some people love their dogs in a manner not at all con-

* I have been told lately that Arab horses are capable of strong affection for their masters, which, if true, may have been the origin of the popular belief.

ducive to the dogs' true happiness and welfare. I knew a lady and gentleman who loved their dog so much that he had a chair at the dinner-table, and slept at night (he was a large retriever) *in* the same bed with his master and mistress. I had the honour of sitting opposite to him at dinner, and was much edified by his well-bred manners. He ate soberly from a plate, like the rest of us. But it is not a kindness to pamper animals of any kind; the true way to be kind to animals is to order their living in every way that they may be cheerful and healthy through their allotted span of life, and we ought not to hesitate about putting them to death when infirmities make existence a burden. So with reference to animals slaughtered for our use, there can be no moral hesitation if only the most merciful death is chosen. It is wrong to bleed calves to death slowly, as is done in England to have the veal white; it is wrong to tear out the eyes of rabbits while yet living, as is done in some parts of France from a notion that the meat is better for it; it is wrong to give geese a liver complaint in order to make Strasbourg pies; but a true *gourmet* will hesitate at no cruelty if it procures him a perceptible increase in the delicate delight of tasting. As to that great horrible question of vivisection, which men of science do really practise much more than is commonly suspected, the discoveries effected by it have prevented, they say, much suffering, but the doubt remains whether a merciful end can justify means so frightfully merciless. The young veterinary surgeons at Maisons-Alfort do actually learn to operate by practising on living horses, which are saved from the knacker for that purpose; and the same science which inflicts tortures worse than those of the Inquisition prolongs the misery of the victims by the most solicitous care in the intervals between one operation and another. Finally, after from twenty to sixty operations, the animals die from sheer inability to endure any more torture; and still the sky is bright over Maisons-Alfort, and the houses are pretty and fanciful, and the gardens sweetly luxuriant, and there are arbours for pleasant shade where the well-to-do messieurs and dames sit sipping their coffee and cognac. A pretty place in the summer, but the hell of horses, punished for no sin!

CHAPTER II.

DOGS.

THERE is a little skull amongst the bones I have collected for the study of anatomy, which any slightly scientific person would at once recognise as that of a dog. It is a beautiful little skull, finely developed, and one sees at a glance that the animal, when it was alive, must have possessed more than ordinary intelligence. The scientific lecturer would consider it rather valuable as an illustration of cranial structure in the higher animals; he might compare it with the skull of a crocodile, and deduce conclusions as to the manifest superiority of the canine brain.

To me this beautiful little example of Divine construction may be a teacher of scientific truths, but it is also a great deal more than that. My memory clothes it with mobile muscles and skin, covered with fine, short hair, in patches of white and yellow. Where another sees only hollow sockets in which lurk perpetual shadows, I can see bright eyes wherein the sunshine played long ago, just as it plays in the topaz depths of some clear northern rivulet. I see the ears too, though the skull has none; and the ears listen and the eyes gaze with an infinite love and longing.

She was the friend of my boyhood, reader, the companion of a thousand rambles, and when she died my boyhood was dead also and became part of the irrecoverable past. There is an indentation in the bone, due to an accident. How well I remember all about that accident! How tenderly we nursed her, how glad we were when she got well again and followed me according to her wont! I wonder how many miles we have travelled together, she and I, along the banks of our own stream and out on the purple moors!

Of course the reader cannot be expected to care very much about a poor little terrier that only loved its young master, as all dogs will, by reason of the instinct that is in them, and died more than eighteen years ago. I am willing to believe that millions of dogs have been as good as she was, and a great deal more valuable in the market, but no skull in the best natural history collections in Europe could tempt me to part with this. Every year makes the relic more precious, since every year certain recollections gradually fade, and this helps me to recover them. You may think that it is a questionable taste to keep so ghastly a reminder. It does not seem ghastly to me, but is only as the dried flower that we treasure in some sacred book. When I think by how much devoted affection this bony tenement was once inhabited, it seems to me still a most fair and beautiful dwelling. The prevailing idea that reigned there was the image of me, her master. Shall I scorn this ivory cell in which my own picture had ever the place of honour?

Many a man past the middle of life remembers with a quite peculiar and especial tenderness that one dog which was the dear companion of his boyhood. No other canine friend can ever be to us exactly what that one was; and here let me venture to observe that the comparative shortness of the lives of dogs is the only imperfection in the relation between them and us. If they had lived to threescore years and ten, man and dog might have travelled through life together, but as it is we must either have a succession of affections, or else, when the first is buried in its early grave, live in a chill condition of doglessness. The certainty of early death is added to the possibility of accident. I had a dog of great gifts, exceptionally intelligent, who would obey a look where another needed an order, and of rare beauty both of colour and form. One evening in the twilight we went out together, and, as cruel fate would have it, I crossed a valley where there was a deep and rapid stream. Rapid and deep it was, yet not much wider than the Strid at Bolton, and there was a mill and a narrow rustic bridge. My poor dog lingered behind a few minutes in the deepening twilight and I called for him in vain. He had tried to leap across between the bridge and the mill, and was hurried to destruction along an irresistible current, between walls of pitiless stone on which he had no hold. I cannot think of that twilight even now without painful sorrow for my poor, imprudent companion. All dogs are worth keeping, but there are very great differences in their natural gifts, and that one had a rare intelligence. He would sit studying his master's face, and had become from careful observation so acute a physiognomist that he read whatever thoughts of mine had any concern for him.

When the theory of selection has done its worst, I still cling to the belief that the relation between dog and man was as much foreseen and intended as that between sun and planet. Man has succeeded in domesticating several other animals, but where else has he found this spirit of unconquerable fidelity? It has not been developed by kind treatment, it has not even been sought for in itself, or made an aim in breeding. Ladies make pets of their dogs, but all the shepherds I see around me pay them in kicks, and curses, and starvation. What does the obscure member of a pack of foxhounds know of his master's love? As much as a Prussian private in the rifle-pit knew of the tender heart of Moltke. I have seen a great deal of the life of the French peasantry, but never to this day have I seen a peasant caress his dog otherwise than with a stick or a wooden shoe. There is a well-known picture, by Decamps, called 'The Kennel,' which represents a huntsman visiting his hounds, and he is lashing with a ponderous whip. Thousands of dogs, whole generations of them, have known man in no other character than that of a merciless commander, punishing the slightest error without pity, yet bestowing no reward.

There are countries where the dogs are never fed, where they are left to pick up a bare existence amongst the vilest refuse, and where they walk like gaunt images of famine, living skeletons, gnawing dry sticks in the wintry moonlight, doing Nature's scavenger-work like rats. Yet in every one of these miserable creatures beats the noble canine heart—that heart whose depths of devotion have never yet been sounded to the bottom; that heart which forgets all our cruelty, but not the smallest evidence of our kindness. If these poor animals had not been made to love us, what excellent reasons they would have had for hating us! Their love has not been developed by care and culture, like the nourishing ears of wheat; but it rises like warm, natural springs, where man has done nothing either to obtain them or to deserve them.

I please myself with the thought that every man is, or may be if he will, a centre round which many kinds of affection press with gently sustaining forces. Let us not undervalue the love which rises up to us from below, bathing our feet in warmth. Only the love of animals, and that of children whilst they are still quite young, is absolutely free from criticism. All our contemporaries criticise us; even our wives do in their hearts, and our sons in their adolescence. The man in his family lives in a glass case, and cannot quite withdraw himself. He is surrounded by more affection than the bachelor, but he incurs in a minor degree that amenability to criticism which is the penalty of a prime minister. The criticism may not be openly expressed, but so soon as he acts independently of the family opinion about his duties he feels that it is there. It is exceedingly salutary, no doubt; it keeps us in the path of duty and dignity; it saves us from many aberrations. And still, upon the whole, we know ourselves to be such lamentably imperfect characters, that we long for an affection altogether ignorant of our faults. Heaven has accorded this to us in the uncritical canine attachment. Women love in us their own exalted ideals, and to live up to the ideal standard is sometimes rather more than we are altogether able to manage; children in their teens find out how clumsy and ignorant we are, and do not quite unreservedly respect us; but our dogs adore us without a suspicion of our shortcomings. There is only one exception, but this is a grave one, and must not on any account be forgotten. A good sporting dog has always an intense contempt for a bad sportsman, so that a man who cannot shoot with a decent degree of skill does best, like a miserable amateur violinist, to abstain from practising altogether.

There are thousands of anecdotes illustrating the wonderful affection which dogs bear to their masters, and as the world goes on thousands of other examples will be recorded, but no one will ever know the full marvel of that immense love and devotion. It is inexhaustible, like the beauty of what is most beautiful in nature, like the glory of sunsets and the rich abundance of that natural loveliness which poets and artists can never quite reveal. We do not know the depth of it even in the dogs we have always with us. I have one who is neither so intelligent nor so affectionate as others I have known, and to my human ignorance it seemed that he did not love me very much. But once, when I had been away for weeks, his melancholy longing, of which he had said nothing to anybody, burst out in a great passionate crisis. He howled and clamoured for admission into my dressing-room, pulled down my old things from their pegs, dragged them into a corner, and flung himself upon them, wailing long and wildly where he lay, till a superstitious fear came on all the house like the forerunner of evil tidings. Who can tell what long broodings, unexpressed, had preceded this passionate outburst ? Many a dark hour had he passed in silent desolation, wondering at that inexplicable absence, till at length the need for me became so urgent that he must touch some cloth that I had worn.

We know not the heart-memory which these animals possess, the long-retaining, tender recollection, all bound up with their love. A dog was bereaved of his master and afterwards became old and blind, passing the dark evening of his existence sadly in the same corner, which he hardly ever quitted. One day came a step like that of his lost master, and he suddenly left his place. The man who had just entered wore ribbed stockings; the old dog had lost his scent and referred at once to the stockings that he remembered rubbing his face against them. Believing that his master had returned after those weary years of absence, he gave way to the most extravagant delight. The man spoke, the momentary illusion was dispelled, the dog went sadly back to his place, lay wearily down, and died.

These little anecdotes, and there are many such, give us glimpses of what is permanent in the canine heart. We think that dogs are demonstrative, but they have regrets of which they tell us nothing. It is likely that the old blind dog, coiled up in his corner day and night, mournfully cherished the recollection of his lost master, thinking of him when the people in the house little suspected those yearnings of melancholy retrospect. There is nothing in nature so sad as that obscure despair. The dog is high enough in the scale of being to feel the regrets of absence in all their bitterness, yet not high enough to have his anxieties relieved by any word of explanation. Whether his master has gone to the next country, or across the sea, or to Heaven, he has no possible means of ascertaining—he only feels the long sorrow of separation, the aching of the solitary heart, the weariness of hope deferred, the anxiety that is never set at rest.

So great is their power of loving that we cannot help assigning to dogs—not formally, but in our inward estimates—a place distinct from the brute creation generally. They are not mere animals, like sheep and oxen, that may be slaughtered as a matter of ordinary business without awakening regret. To kill a dog is always felt to be a sort of murder; it is the destruction of a beautiful though not immortal spirit, and the destruction is the more lamentable for its very completeness. When I was a boy I remember crossing a stream in Lancashire just as a workman came to the same place followed by a sharp-looking little brown terrier dog. It went snuffing about under the roots as such little dogs will, and then the man whistled and it came to him at full speed. He caressed it, spoke to it very kindly but very sadly, and then began to tie a great stone to its neck. 'What are you doing that for?' I asked. 'Because I cannot afford to pay the dog-tax, and nobody else shall have my little Jip.' Then he threw it into the stream. The water was not deep, and it was perfectly clear, so that we saw the painful struggles of the poor little terrier till it became insensible, and we were both fixed to the spot by a sort of fascination. At last the man turned away with a pale hard face, suffering, in that moment, more than he cared to show, and I went my way carrying with me an impression which is even now as strong as ever it was. I felt that what I had witnessed was a murder. Many years after, I shot a dog of my own (a magnificent blood-hound mastiff) because he was an irreclaimable sheep-killer; but the revolver I did it with instantly became so hateful that I could not bear the sight of it, and never fired it afterwards. Even now, if he could but be raised from the dead, how gladly would I welcome him, how securely would I rely for perfect forgiveness on his noble canine magnanimity! No, these creatures are not common brutes, they are our most trusting friends, and we cannot take away their lives without a treacherous betrayal of that trust.

A word came under my pen just now by accident which belongs quite peculiarly to the canine nature. It does not belong to all dogs; there are little breeds which seem to be almost destitute of it, but all the nobler breeds are magnanimous. As we are told to go to the ant to learn industry, so we may go to the dog for an example of magnanimity. The finest touches of it in his nature are not so much in the absolute insensibility to offence as in his courteous willingness to attribute offences which he cannot possibly overlook to some pardonable mistake of yours, or blameable error of his own. Even when most severely punished he never seems to doubt the justice of the punishment, but takes it in the finest possible temper, as a perfect Christian would take chastisement at the hand of God. And pray observe that with all this submissiveness, with all this readiness to forget your severity and to bask in the first gleam of the sunshine of your clemency, there is not the faintest trace of snobbishness in his nature. The dog is faithful to his master even when he gets hardly anything out of him. It is said that every dog is an aristocrat, because rich men's dogs cannot endure beggars and their rags, and are civil only to well-dressed visitors. But the truth is that, from sympathy for his master, the dog always sees humanity very much from his master's point of view. The poor man's dog does not dislike the poor. I may go much farther than this, and venture to assert that a dog who has lived with you for years will make the same distinction between your visitors that you make yourself, inwardly, notwithstanding the apparent uniformity of your outward politeness. My dog is very civil to people I like, but he is savage to those I dislike, whatever the tailor may have done to lend them external charms. I know not how he discovers these differences in my feelings, except it be by overhearing remarks when the guests are gone.

How much do dogs really understand of our language? Perhaps a good deal more than we generally imagine. Please observe that in learning a foreign tongue you arrive at a certain stage where most of what the foreign people say is broadly intelligible to you, and yet you cannot express yourself at all. Very young children understand a great deal before they are able to express themselves in words. Even horses,—and horses are incomparably less intelligent than dogs,—understand a complete vocabulary of orders. May not a dog of ability enter, to some extent, into the meaning of spoken language even though he may never be able to use it? Without giving the reins to imagination, it may be presumed that some dogs know at laast the names of different people, and may take note of the manner, cordial or otherwise, in which we pronounce them. Whatever they may know of spoken language, it is quite clear that they understand the language of manner, and have a very delicate appreciation of human behaviour.

Besides the love which the dog has for his master, and for him alone, he has his friendships and acquaintances with humanity. And as a married man may quite innocently establish friendships with ladies whom he likes and respects, so the most faithful of dogs may have kindly feelings for men who stand in no nearer relation to him than that of acquaintance. All my friends' dogs are polite acquaintances of mine, and conduct themselves with becoming courtesy. One fat lady is the happy owner of the tiniest creature that ever aspired to the dignity of dog-hood, and as our acquaintance seemed to have ripened into an intimacy, I invited Bellona (for such was her warlike name) to share with me the perilous pleasures of a canoe-voyage. This, however, was presuming too far, and at the first landing she deserted the ship and fled homewards, like a frightened rabbit, across the fields. There are limits to the *liaisons*. On the other hand, I once invited a friend's dog to accompany me on an equestrian excursion, and he followed my horse for eighty miles, enjoying the change of scene and the meals we shared together. It has also happened to me, to send a formal written invitation to a friend's dog to come and stay with me for a fortnight. He accepted the invitation, came by railway, and behaved himself in the most charming manner, renewing our ancient friendship with the most amicable demonstrations. It is needless to add that he was received with all the honour that the laws of hospitality exact. Sometimes a dog will forget a mere friend, though he never forgets his master. I remember crossing a public square in winter, at midnight, and seeing a poor lost dog that I recognised as an old acquaintance. There could be no mistake about it, she had every physical mark and sign of the gentle little creature that I knew, the only cause of doubt was that she could not be induced to give the slightest,—no, not the very slightest, sign of recognition. I caught her and carried her in my arms to the hotel, held her up to the light, examined every mark —the body was all there, but where was the friendly heart that used to beat with gladness when we met, far in the quiet country, in the lanes and fields about her home? I put her down, and she immediately escaped and was lost again in the windings of the streets. The next morning I went early to the farm she lived at and inquired if she were lost. Yes, it was true, she had been lost in the confusion of the fair. Later she found her own way back again and behaved to me as amiably as ever. Probably, in the town, the sight of so many people had bewildered her till she could not recognise a friend, but a dog knows his master everywhere.

One of my dog-friends knew me, however, and behaved well to me under very trying circumstances indeed, for he was suffering from hydrophobia. I was perfectly aware myself of the terrible nature of his ailment, but he came to me, and put his head between my knees, like a sick child, and I caressed it out of very profound pity. When the paroxysms became violent as the disease advanced, the dog still controlled himself, and his master took him in his arms and carried the poor beast up into a vacant garret and locked the door. Then he made a hole in the thin brick partition, and with a small rifle, of the kind used for rook-shooting, put an end to an existence that had become intolerable. Of all the ills that flesh is heir to there is not one so terrible as this mysterious madness. Every year human victims perish in its unutterable agony. Scarcely less terrible than the disease itself is the awful apprehension of it for weeks and months after the poisonous bite. A young man died last year within a little distance of my home, and the dog that killed him had bitten three other persons, who from that time till now have been expecting the fearful symptoms. Think what it must be to pass month after month with the horrible suggestion incessantly recurring, 'Am I to go mad to-morrow?' Even these fears do not deter heroic natures from the performance of what they consider to be their duty. A French boy, in a locality well known to me, was taking his little sister to school. In the narrow path they met a dog, and the dog was raging mad. It bit the boy, but he seized it by the collar and held it, calling to his sister to escape. The girl escaped, the boy died of hydrophobia. A similar case occurred at another spot I know, where a wolf attacked a man and a woman. The wolf happened to be suffering from hydrophobia, and bit the man, who died. The woman escaped by getting into a tree. A healthy wolf may be an unpleasant animal to meet in forest-paths, but a mad one is much worse. A friend of mine witnessed a terrible encounter between a blacksmith and a mad dog. A whole village was in consternation on account of a great dog that was rushing about in a state of very advanced hydrophobia, when the blacksmith went forth armed with a large hammer and nothing else, to meet the common enemy. He walked in the middle of the village street, when at length the beast came, going on in a straight line. The first hammer-blow missed its aim, the hammer swung clear, but the dog stopped, and it seemed as if the dreaded poisonous bite was not to be avoided; however, the smith recovered his position rapidly enough to deliver a second blow, this time fatal, before the animal touched him. He had shown great courage whilst the danger lasted, but as soon as it was over he fainted.

Let us change the subject, and quit this horrible topic, hydrophobia, with its hopeless and unimaginable miseries. In all the grim catalogue of diseases surely this is the most awful! Nothing more clearly proves the necessity of dogs to men, or the strength of the love we bear to these poor creatures, than our persistence in keeping so near to us the source of so frightful a calamity. Every year the newspapers tell us the same tale of its victims; how they were bitten; how the madness broke forth at last and led them to the inevitable agony. We cannot realise those sufferings; we cannot by any effort of sympathy or imagination bring ourselves to understand what flowing water, to us so sweet a refreshment, may be to an organisation revolutionised by irresistible disease. We only know the *reality* of the suffering, though its nature and origin are mysteries.

CHAPTER III.

DOGS (*continued*).

WOULD that dogs could communicate their health and energy to us, as they can their fearful malady! They possess in a much higher degree than man, the power of storing up energy in times of repose, and keeping it for future use. A dog spends his spare time in absolute rest, and is able to endure great drains of energy on due occasion. He lies idly by the fire, and looks so lazy, that it seems as if nothing could make him stir, yet at a sign from his master he will get up and go anywhere, without hesitation about the distance. In old age dogs know that they have not any longer these great reserves of force, and decline to follow their masters who go out on horseback, but will still gladly follow them on any merely pedestrian excursion, well knowing the narrow limits of human strength and endurance. Dogs in the prime of life accomplish immense distances, not without fatigue, for these efforts exhaust them for the moment, but they have such great recuperative power that they entirely recover by rest. I know a very small dog that was given by his master to a friend who lived sixty miles off. His new proprietor carried him in the inside of a coach; but the next morning the little animal was in his old home again, having found his way across country, and a most fatiguing and bewildering country too, covered with dense forests and steep hills. Has the reader ever observed how much swifter dogs are than their behaviour would lead one to imagine? Here is an illustration of what I mean. I know a very rapid coach which is always preceded by a middling-sized dog of no particular breed. Well, this dog amuses itself within a yard of the horses' hoofs, turning round, leaping, looking at other vehicles, snapping at other dogs, barking at its own and other horses, and leading, in a word, exactly the same kind of life as if it were amusing itself in the inn-yard before starting. Now, consider a little the amazing perfection of organisation, the readiness and firmness of nerve, required for motions so complicated as these, and the bodily energy, too, necessary to keep them up, not for a few yards, but mile after mile as the coach rattles along the road! One false step, one second of delay, and the dog would be under the hoofs of the horses, yet he plays as children play on the sea-shore before the slowly-advancing tide. With the dog's energy, and a wiser economy of it, a man could run a hundred miles without an interval of rest.

We make use of the delicate faculty of scent possessed by these animals to aid us in the chase, and are so accustomed to rely upon it that its marvellousness escapes

F

attention. But we have no physical faculty so exquisite as this. It is clear that the dog's opinions about odours must be widely different from ours, for he endures very strong smells which to us are simply intolerable, and positively enjoys what we abominate; but as for true delicacy of nerve, which I take to be the power of detecting what is most faint, we cannot presume to the least comparison with him. Every one who has gathered wild plants knows what an immense variety of odours arise from the plants upon the ground—this is the first complication; next upon that (though we cannot detect it) are traced in all directions different lines of scent laid down by the passage of animals and men—this is the second complication. Well, across these labyrinths of misleading or disturbing odours the dog follows the one scent he cares for at the time (notwithstanding its incessant alteration by mixture) as easily as we should follow a scarlet thread on a green field. If he were only sensitive to the one scent he followed, the marvel would be much reduced, but he knows many different odours, and selects amongst them the one that interests him at the time. The only human faculty comparable to this is the perception of delicate tints by the most accomplished and gifted painters, but here I believe that the intellectual powers of man do much in the education of the eye. No young child could ever colour, though its eye were physically perfect, and colouring power comes only through study, which is always more or less a definitely mental operation. The dog can hardly be said to study scents, though long practice through unnumbered generations may have given refinement and precision to his faculty.

In speaking of a power of this kind, possessed by another animal, we are liable to mistakes which proceed from our constant reference to our own human perceptions. We think, for instance, that the odour of thyme is strong, whilst for us the scent left by an animal in its passage may be so faint as to be imperceptible; but scents that are strong for us may be faint for dogs, and *vice versâ*. Odours are not positive but relative, they are sensations simply, and the same cause does not produce the same sensation in different organisms. A dog rolls himself on carrion, and unreflecting people think this a proof of a disgustingly bad taste on his part; but it is evident that the carrion gives him a sensation entirely different from that which it produces in ourselves. I know a man who says that to him the odour of any cheese whatever, even the freshest and soundest, is disgusting beyond the power of language to express; is it not evident that cheese produces in him a sensation altogether different from what it causes in most of us? The smell and taste of dogs may be not the less refined and delicate that they differ widely from our own. The *cause* of the most horrible of all smells in my own experience is a mouse, but the same cause produces, it is probable, an effect altogether different upon the olfactory nerves of cats. These mysteries of sensation, in other beings, are quite unfathomable, and our human theories about delicacy of taste are not worth a moment's attention. The dog is quite as good an authority on these questions as the best of us.

I cannot think that it is very surprising that dogs should *remember* odours well, since odours so long retain the power of awakening old associations in ourselves. I distinctly remember the odour of every house that was familiar to me in boyhood, and should recognise it at once. In the same way dogs know the scent of a well-known footstep, even after long separation. An officer returned home after the Franco-German war and did not meet his dog. After his arrival he watched for the dog through the window. He saw it at last in a state of intense excitement, following his track at full speed, never raising its nostrils from the ground, and then came the joyful meeting—the scent had been recognised from the beginning, even in a much-frequented street.

Innumerable anecdotes might be collected to illustrate the reasoning power of dogs. A certain lawyer, a neighbour of mine, has a dog that guards his money when clients come into the office. There are two or three pieces of furniture, and sometimes it happens that the lawyer puts money into one or another of these, temporarily, the dog always watching him, and guarding that particular piece of furniture where the money lies. In this instance the dog had gradually become aware, from his master's manner, that money was an object of more than ordinary solicitude; in fact, he had been set to guard coin left upon the table. I refrain from repeating current stories about the sagacity of dogs, because, although many of them are perfectly credible, they are naturally exaggerated in transmission. I happened to be in a railway carriage where several sportsmen were telling marvellous stories about their dogs, whilst an elderly man sat in his corner and said nothing. At last he spoke: 'Gentlemen,' he said, 'all this is very remarkable, but I have a dog who is still more wonderful than the most wonderful of yours. For example, you see that river; well, if I were to throw a sovereign into that river, my dog would immediately plunge in *and bring me the change in silver.*' 'Really, sir, you surprise me!' said one of the sportsmen, not quick enough to see the intended sarcasm. Auguste Villemot used to tell a story with a like intention about a blind man's dog in Paris, which, after receiving money for its master, continued the business after his death, and accumulated a considerable fortune.

Let me add a few words about the treatment of these faithful friends of ours. I need scarcely protest against the ignorant and stupid mutilation of dogs by cutting their ears and tail. From the artistic point of view this is barbarous in the last degree, because it spoils their instruments of expression. It is like cutting out the tongue of a human being. There is a poor dog near me whose tail has been amputated at the very root, and the consequence is that he cannot tell me the half of what he thinks. Sir Edwin Landseer was greatly pleased to meet with a dog-seller who would not mutilate his animals, for the reason that 'Sir Edwin Landseer did not approve of it.' In a smaller way every one of us may exercise the same merciful influence, and I earnestly request every reader of these lines to discourage openly the mutilation of dogs and other animals. It is an evil very generally prevalent and of very long standing, and it is due to the desire for improving nature, for turning natural things as far as possible into artificial things, which is instinctive in mankind and leads to the most useful results; but this is one of its false directions. People who are only partially civilised do not see where they ought to respect nature, and where to make alterations; so they cannot leave anything alone. The highest civilisation does little more than remove impediments to perfect natural growth, and accepts the divine ideals as the ideals towards which it strives. The best practical way to prevent people from mutilating dogs is, not to reason on the subject (for reason is far too weak to contend against custom), but to employ ridicule. I make it a rule to tell everybody who keeps a mutilated dog, that his dog is both ugly and absurd; and if a good many people hear me, so much the better. There is another very common sort of cruelty to dogs, which might easily be prevented by the exercise of a little common sense. Many dog-owners, especially kind-hearted but weak-minded ladies, are accustomed to injure their pets by giving them too much food and too little exercise. Pampered dogs are certainly not the happiest dogs. Only look at them! Can a creature which was intended by nature for the most exuberant activity be said to enjoy life when it can hardly waddle across a carpet? There is not an honest doctor who, after examining the teeth and breath, and observing the digestion of these wretched martyrs to mistaken kindness, will not tell you that they have no genuine health, and without that neither dog nor man can be happy. If you really care about making your dog happy, the way to do so is both extremely simple and perfectly well known. Feed him regularly and moderately, see that his bodily functions go as they ought to do, and vary his diet when necessary. Above all, give him plenty of exercise, take him out with you into the fields and woods—that is what he most enjoys. Keep him under a strict and wholesome discipline, for dogs are happiest, as men are, when wisely and steadily governed. Our caresses ought to be reserved as a reward, or a recognition, not given continually till the dog is weary of them. In the same way, besides the regular food, we may give occasionally little morsels out of kindness, because he values the kindness, just as we like a cigar that a friend gives us out of his own case. His happiness, like our own, is best promoted by activity, by temperance, by obedience to duty, and by the sort of affection that is not incompatible with perfect dignity, of which every noble dog has his full share.

But however healthy and happy a dog may be, there comes a time at last when the gladness fades out of his life. I see with sorrow that my poor old Tom feels obliged to decline to follow me now when I go out on horseback. This is one of the first symptoms of old age, and he does not hear so well or see so well as formerly. Still, on a bright morning, when we go out in the woods together, he is quite himself again, apparently, and the old activity revives. It is that last renewal of summer which precedes the frosts of autumn, that after-glow in the western sky which is so swiftly followed by the leaden greys of night. One of my neighbours has an old dog that can neither hear nor see, and passes the dark, silent days in an arm-chair which has been given to him for the comfort of his age. One sound is audible by him still, and one only—a little shrill silver whistle that he has obeyed from puppyhood till now. It is one of the most pathetic sights I ever witnessed, when the master comes and sounds the piercing call. The inert thing in the arm-chair becomes galvanised with sudden life, tumbles down upon the floor, crawls towards the sound, finds the beloved hand, and licks it. They pass whole evenings together still, that gentle master and his poor old friend. And still in that dark decrepitude beats the heart of inextinguishable love.

It happens very fortunately for modern art, that dogs have not only the interest of character and intelligence, which is what the general public cares most about, but also a rich variety of form and colour and texture, abounding in striking contrasts, delighting the eye of the artist whilst he is at work, and permitting him to make good pictures. Although dogs have been more or less painted and carved since men used brush and chisel, they have never held so important a position in art as they do now. The modern love of incident in pictures, the modern delight in what has been aptly called 'literary interest' as distinguished from the pure pleasure of the eyes, naturally induce us to give a very high place to dogs, which more than all other animals are capable of awakening an interest of this kind. The dog is so close to man, so intimately associated with his life, both in the field and in the house, that he becomes a sharer in many of its incidents, and the painter scarcely needs a pretext for introducing him. In such a picture, for example, as the 'Order of Release' (by Millais), the dog has his due importance as a member of the family, and the painter does not ignore the canine gladness and affection. And so in the illustration, by the same artist, of that charming old Scottish song, 'There is nae luck about the house,' the dog is first out of doors to go and meet the gudeman. In Landseer's 'Shepherd's Chief Mourner' the dog is alone in his lamentation, and yet we feel that the bereaved creature is in the place that is his by a natural right, by right of long service, of constant companionship, of humble faithful friendship and deep love. You paint a portrait of Sir Walter Scott, why not introduce Maida? —of young Lord Byron, why not put brave Boatswain by his side? These creatures rejoice with us in our sports and at our festivals, and they mourn for us in the hour of that separation which religion and science agree to consider eternal. We, too, mourn for them, when they leave us, and pass from the fulness of life into the abyss of nothingness. There may be human relatives for whom you will wear funereal hatbands, for whom you will blacken the borders of envelopes and cards, and who, nevertheless, will not be regretted with that genuine sorrow that the death of a dog will bring. Many a tear is shed every year in England for the loss of these humble friends, and many a heart has been relieved by the welcome tidings, 'There's life in the old dog yet.'

CHAPTER IV.

CATS.

ONE evening before dinner-time the present writer had occasion to go into a dining-room where the cloth was already laid, the glasses all in their places on the sideboard and table, and the lamp and candles lighted. A cat, which was a favourite in the house, finding the door ajar, entered softly after me, and began to make a little exploration after his manner. I have a fancy for watching animals when they think they are not observed, so I affected to be entirely absorbed in the occupation which detained me there, but took note of the cat's proceedings without in any way interrupting them. The first thing he did was to jump upon a chair, and thence upon the sideboard. There was a good deal of glass and plate upon that piece of furniture, but nothing as yet which, in the cat's opinion, was worth purloining: so he brought all his paws together on the very edge of the board, the two forepaws in the middle, the others on both sides, and sat balancing himself in that attitude for a minute or two, whilst he contemplated the long glittering vista of the table. As yet there was not an atom of anything eatable upon it, but the cat probably thought he might as well ascertain whether this were so or not by a closer inspection, for with a single spring he cleared the abyss and alighted noiselessly on the table-cloth. He walked all over it and left no trace; he passed amongst the slender glasses, fragile-stemmed, like air-bubbles cut in half and balanced on spears of ice; yet he disturbed nothing, broke nothing, anywhere. When his inspection was over he slipped out of sight, having been perfectly inaudible from the beginning, so that a blind person could only have suspected his visit by that mysterious sense which makes the blind aware of the presence of another creature.

This little scene reveals one remarkable characteristic of the feline nature, the innate and exquisite refinement of its behaviour. It would be infinitely difficult, probably even impossible, to communicate a delicacy of this kind to any animal by teaching. The cat is a creature of most refined and subtle perceptions naturally. Why should she tread so carefully? It is not from fear of offending her master and incurring punishment, but because to do so is in conformity with her own ideal of behaviour; exactly as a lady would feel vexed with herself if she broke anything in her own drawing-room, though no one would blame her *maladresse* and she would never feel the loss.

The contrast in this respect between cats and other animals is very striking. I will not wrong the noble canine nature so far as to say that it has no delicacy, but its delicacy is not of this kind, not in actual touch, as the cat's is. The motions of the cat, being always governed by the most refined sense of touch in the animal world, are typical in quite a perfect way of what we call tact in the human world. And as a man who has tact exercises it on all occasions for his own satisfaction, even when there is no positive need for it, so a cat will walk daintily and observantly everywhere, whether amongst the glasses on a dinner-table or the rubbish in a farm-yard.

It is easy to detract from the admirableness of this delicate quality in the cat by a reference to the necessities of her life in a wild state. Any one not much disposed to enter into imaginative sentimentalities about animals might say to us, 'What you admire so much as a proof of ladylike civilisation in the cat, is rather an evidence that she has retained her savage habits. When she so carefully avoids the glasses on the dinner-table she is not thinking of her behaviour as a dependent on civilised man, but acting in obedience to hereditary habits of caution in the stealthy chase, which is the natural accomplishment of her species. She will stir no branch of a shrub lest her fated bird escape her, and her feet are noiseless that the mouse may not know of her coming.' This, no doubt, would be a probable account of the origin of that fineness of touch and movement which belongs to cats, but the fact of that fineness remains. In all the domestic animals, and in man himself, there are instincts and qualities still more or less distinctly traceable to a savage state, and these qualities are often the very basis of civilisation itself. That which in the wild cat is but the stealthy cunning of the hunter, is refined in the tame one into a habitual gentleness often very agreeable to ladies, who dislike the boisterous demonstrations of the dog and his incorrigible carelessness.

This quality of extreme caution, which makes the cat avoid obstacles that a dog would dash through without a thought, makes her at the same time somewhat reserved and suspicious in all the relations of her life. If a cat has been allowed to run half-wild this suspicion can never be overcome. There was a numerous population of cats in this half-wild state for some years in the garrets of my house. Some of these were exceedingly fine, handsome animals, and I very much wished to get them into the rooms we inhabited, and so domesticate them; but all my blandishments were useless. The nearest approach to success was in the case of a superb white-and-black animal, who, at last, would come to me occasionally, and permit me to caress his head, because I scratched him behind the ears. Encouraged by this measure of confidence, I went so far on one occasion as to lift him a few inches from the ground: on which he behaved himself very much like a wild cat just trapped in the woods, and for some days after it was impossible even to get near him. He never came down-stairs in a regular way, but communicated with the outer world by means of roofs and trees, like the other untameable creatures in the garrets. On returning home after an absence I sought him vainly, and have never encountered him since.

This individual lived on the confines of civilisation,

and it is possible that his tendency to friendliness might have been developed into a feeling more completely trustful by greater delicacy and care. I happened to mention him to an hotel-keeper who was unusually fond of animals, and unusually successful in winning their affections. He told me that his own cats were remarkable for their uncommon tameness, being very much petted and caressed, and constantly in the habit of seeing numbers of people who came to the hotel, and he advised me to try a kitten of his breed. This kitten, from hereditary civilisation, behaved with the utmost confidence from the beginning, and, with the exception of occasional absences for his own purposes, has lived with me regularly enough. In winter he generally sleeps upon my dog, who submits in patience; and I have often found him on horseback in the stable, not from any taste for equestrianism, but simply because a horse-cloth is a perpetual warmer when there is a living horse beneath it.

All who have written upon cats are unanimous in the opinion that their caressing ways bear reference simply to themselves. My cat loves the dog and horse exactly with the tender sentiment we have for foot-warmers and railway rugs during a journey in the depth of winter, nor have I ever been able to detect any worthier feeling towards his master. Ladies are often fond of cats, and pleasantly encourage the illusion that they are affectionate; it is said too that very intellectual men have often a liking for the same animal. In both these cases the attachment seems to be due more to certain other qualities of the cat than to any strength of sentiment on his part. Of all animals that we can have in a room with us, the cat is the least disturbing. Dogs bring so much dirt into houses that many ladies have a positive horror of them; squirrels leap about in a manner highly dangerous to the ornaments of a drawing-room; whilst monkeys are so incorrigibly mischievous that it is impossible to tolerate them, notwithstanding the nearness of the relationship. But you may have a cat in the room with you without anxiety about anything except eatables. He will rob a dish if he can get at it, but he will not, except by the rarest of accidents, displace a sheet of paper or upset an inkstand. The presence of a cat is positively soothing to a student, as the presence of a quiet nurse is soothing to the irritability of an invalid. It is agreeable to feel that you are not absolutely alone, and it seems to you, as you work, as if the cat took care that all her movements should be noiseless, purely out of consideration for your comfort. Then, if you have time to caress her, you know that there will be purring responses, and why inquire too closely into the sincerity of her gratitude? There have been instances of people who surrounded themselves with cats; old maids have this fancy sometimes, which is intelligible, because old maids delight in having objects on which to lavish their inexhaustible kindness, and their love of neatness and comfort is in harmony with the neat habits of these comfort-appreciating creatures. A dog on velvet is evidently out of place, he would be as happy on clean straw, but a cat on velvet does not awaken any sense of the incongruous. It is more difficult to understand how men of business ever take to cats. A well-known French politician, who certainly betrayed nothing feminine in his speeches, was so fond of cats that it was impossible to dine peaceably at his house on account of four licensed feline marauders which promenaded upon the dinner-table, helping themselves to everything, and jumping about the shoulders of the guests. It may be observed that in Paris cats frequently appear upon the table in another shape. I once stayed in a house not very far from the great triumphal arch; and from my window, at certain hours of the day, might be observed a purveyor of dead cats who supplied a small cheap restaurant in a back street. I never went to eat at the restaurant, but ascertained that it had a certain reputation for a dish supposed to be made of rabbits. During the great siege, many Parisians who may frequently have eaten cat without knowing it (as you also may perchance have done, respected reader) came to eat cat with clear knowledge of the true nature of the feast, and they all seem to agree that it was very good. Our prejudices about the flesh we use for food are often inconsistent, the most reasonable one seems to be a preference for vegetable feeders, yet we eat lobsters and pike. The truth is that nobody who eats even duck can consistently have a horror of cat's flesh on the ground of the animal's habits. And although the cat is a carnivorous animal, it has a passionate fondness for certain vegetable substances, delighting in the odour of valerian, and in the taste of asparagus, the former to ecstasy, the latter to downright gluttony.

Since artists cannot conveniently have lions and tigers in their studios, they sometimes like to have cats merely that they may watch the ineffable grace of their motions. Stealthy and treacherous as they are, they have yet a quite peculiar finish of style in action, far surpassing, in certain qualities of manner, the most perfectly-trained action of horses, or even the grace of the roe-deer or the gazelle. All other animals are stiff in comparison with the felines, all other animals have distinctly bodies supported by legs, reminding one of the primitive toy-maker's conception of a quadruped, a cylinder on four sticks, with a neck and head at one end and a tail at the other. But the cat no more recalls this rude anatomy than does a serpent. From the tips of his whiskers to the extremities of tail and claws he is so much living india-rubber. One never thinks of muscles and bones whilst looking at him (*has* he any muscles and bones ?), but only of the reserved electric life that lies waiting under the softness of the fur. What bursts of energy the creature is capable of! I once shut up a half-wild cat in a room and he flew about like a frightened bird, or like leaves caught in a whirlwind. He dashed against the window-panes like sudden hail, ran up the walls like arrested water, and flung himself everywhere with such rapidity that he filled as much space, and filled it almost as dangerously, as twenty flashing swords. And yet this incredibly wild energy is in the creature's quiet habits subdued with an exquisite moderation. The cat always uses precisely the necessary force, other animals roughly employ what strength they happen to possess without reference to the small occasion. One day I watched a young cat playing with a daffodil. She sat on her hind-legs and patted the flower with her paws, first with one paw and then with the other, making the light yellow bell sway from side to side, yet not injuring a petal or a stamen. She took a delight, evidently, in the very delicacy of the exercise, whereas a dog or a horse has no enjoyment of delicacy in his own movements, but acts strongly when he is strong, without calculating whether the force used may not be in great part superfluous. This proportioning of the force to the need is well known to be one of the evidences of refined culture, both in manners and in the fine arts. If animals could speak as fabulists have feigned, the dog would be a blunt, blundering outspoken, honest fellow, but the cat would have the rare talent of never saying a word too much. A hint of the same character is conveyed by the sheathing of the claws, and also by the contractability of the pupil of the eye. The hostile claws are invisible, and are not shown when they are wanted, yet are ever sharp and ready. The eye has a narrow pupil in broad daylight, receiving no more sunshine than is agreeable, but it will gradually expand as twilight falls, and clear vision needs a larger and larger surface. Some of these cat-qualities are very desirable in criticism. The claws of a critic ought to be very sharp, but not perpetually prominent, and his eye ought to see far into rather obscure subjects without being dazzled by plain daylight.

It is odd that, notwithstanding the extreme beauty of cats, their elegance of motion, the variety and intensity of their colour, they should be so little painted by considerable artists. Almost all the pictures of cats which I remember were done by inferior men, often by artists of a very low grade indeed. The reason for this is probably, that although the cat is a refined and very voluptuous animal, it is so wanting in the nobler qualities as to fail in winning the serious sympathies of noble and generous-hearted men. M. Manet once very appropriately introduced a black cat on the bed of a Parisian lorette, and this cat became quite famous for a week or two in all the Parisian newspapers, being also cleverly copied by the caricaturists. No other painted cat ever attracted so much attention, indeed 'Le chat de M. Manet' amused Paris as Athens amused itself with the dog of Alcibiades.

M. Manet's cat had an awful look, and depths of meaning were discoverable in its eyes of yellow flame set in the blackness of the night. There has always been a feeling that a black cat was not altogether 'canny.' Many of us, if we were quite sincere, would confess to a superstition about black cats. They seem to know too much, and is it not written that their ancestors were the companions and accomplices of witches in the times of old? Who can tell what baleful secrets may not have been transmitted through their generations? There can be no doubt that cats know a great deal more than they choose to tell us, though occasionally they may let a secret out in some unguarded moment. Shelley the poet, who had an intense sense of the supernatural, narrates the following history, as he heard it from Mr. G. Lewis:—

'A gentleman on a visit to a friend who lived on the skirts of an extensive forest on the east of Germany lost his way. He wandered for some hours among the trees, when he saw a light at a distance. On approaching it, he was surprised to observe that it proceeded from the interior of a ruined monastery. Before he knocked, he thought it prudent to look through the window. He saw a multitude of cats assembled round a small grave, four of whom were letting down a coffin with a crown upon it. The gentleman, startled at this unusual sight, and imagining that he had arrived among the retreats of fiends or witches, mounted his horse and rode away with the utmost precipitation. He arrived at his friend's house at a late hour, who had sat up for him. On his arrival, his friend questioned as to the cause of the traces of trouble visible on his face. He began to recount his adventure, after much difficulty, knowing that it was scarcely possible that his friends should give faith to his relation. No sooner had he mentioned the coffin with a crown upon it, than his friend's cat, who seemed to have been lying asleep before the fire, leaped up, saying, "Then I am the King of the Cats!" and scrambled up the chimney and was seen no more.'

Now, is not that a remarkable story, proving, at the same time, the attention cats pay to human conversation even when they outwardly seem perfectly indifferent to it, and the monarchical character of their political organisation, which without this incident might have remained for ever unknown to us? This happened, we are told, in eastern Germany; but in our own island, less than a hundred years ago, there remained at least one cat fit to be the ministrant of a sorceress. When Sir Walter Scott visited the Black Dwarf, 'Bowed Davie Ritchie,' the Dwarf said, ' Man, *hae ye ony poo'r ?* ' meaning power of a supernatural kind, and he added solemnly, pointing to a large black cat whose fiery eyes shone in a dark corner of the cottage, 'HE *has poo'r!*' In Scott's place any imaginative person would have more than half believed Davie, as indeed did his illustrious visitor. The ancient Egyptians, who knew as much about magic as the wisest of the moderns, certainly believed that the cat had *poo'r*, or they would not have mummified him with such painstaking conscientiousness. It may easily be imagined, that in times when science did not exist a creature, whose fur emitted lightnings when anybody rubbed it in the dark, must have inspired great awe, and there is really an air of mystery about cats which considerably exercises the imagination. This impression would be intensified in the case of people born with a physical antipathy to cats, and there are such persons. A Captain Logan, of Knockshinnock in Ayrshire, is mentioned in one of the early numbers of *Chambers' Journal* as having this antipathy in the strongest form. He simply could not endure the sight of cat or kitten, and though a tall, strong man, would do anything to escape from the objects of his instinctive and uncontrollable horror, climbing upon chairs if a cat entered the room, and not daring to come down till the creature was removed from his presence. These mysterious repugnances are outside the domain of reason. Many people, not without courage, are seized with involuntary shudderings when they see a snake or a toad; others could not bring themselves to touch a rat, though the rat is one of the cleanliest of animals—not, certainly, as to his food, but his person. It may be presumed that one Mrs. Griggs, who lived, I believe, in Edinburgh, did not share Captain Logan's antipathy, for she kept in her house no less than eighty-six living cats, and had, besides, twenty-eight dead ones in glass cases, immortalised by the art of the taxidermist. If it is true, and it certainly is so in a great measure, that those who love most know most, then Mrs. Griggs would have been a much more competent person to write on cats than the colder-minded author of these chapters. It is wonderful to think how much that good lady must have known of the *loveableness* of cats, of those recondite qualities which may endear them to the human heart!

What a difference in knowledge and feeling concerning cats between Mrs. Griggs and a gamekeeper! The gamekeeper knows a good deal about them too, but it is not exactly affection which has given keenness to *his* observation. He does not see a 'dear sweet pet' in every cat that crosses his woodland paths, but the most destructive of poachers, the worst of 'vermin.' And there can be no doubt that from his point of view the gamekeeper is quite right, even as good Mrs. Griggs may have been from hers. If cats killed game from hunger only, there would be a limit to their depredations, but unfortunately they have the instinct of sport, which sportsmen consider a very admirable quality in themselves, but regard with the strongest disapprobation in other animals. Mr. Frank Buckland says, that when once a cat has acquired the passion for hunting it becomes so strong that it is impossible to break him of it. He knew a cat which had been condemned to death, but the owner begged its life on condition that it should be shut up every night and well fed. The very first night of its incarceration it escaped up the chimney, and was found the next morning, black with soot, in one of the gamekeeper's traps. The keeper easily determines what kind of animal has been committing depredations in his absence. 'Every animal has his own way of killing and eating his prey. The cat always turns the skin *inside out*, leaving tne same reversed like a glove. The weasel and stoat will eat the brain and nibble about the head, and suck the blood. The fox will always leave the legs and hinder parts of a hare or a rabbit; the dog tears his prey to pieces, and eats it "anyhow—all over the place;" the crows and magpies always peck at the eyes before they touch any part of the body.'

'Again,' continues Mr. Frank Buckland, 'let the believer in the innocence of Mrs. Puss listen to the crow of the startled pheasant; he will hear him "tree," as the keeper calls it, and from his safe perch up in a branch again crow as if to summon his protector to his aid. No second summons does the keeper want; he at once runs to the spot, and there, stealing with erect ears, glaring eyes, and limbs collected together, and at a high state of tension, ready for the fatal spring, he sees—what ?—the cat, of course, caught in the very attitude of premeditated poaching.'

This love of sport might perhaps be turned to account if cats were trained as larger felines are trained for the princes of India. A fisherman of Portsmouth, called 'Robinson Crusoe,' made famous by Mr. Buckland, had a cat called 'Puddles,' which overcame the horror of water characteristic of his race, and employed his piscatorial talents in the service of his master:—

'He was the wonderfullest water-cat as ever came out of Portsmouth Harbor was Puddles, and he used to go out a-fishing with me every night. On cold nights he would sit in my lap while I was a-fishing and poke his head out every now and then, or else I would wrap him up in a sail, and make him lay quiet. He'd lay down on me when I was asleep, and if anybody come he'd swear a good one, and have the face off on 'em if they went to touch me; and he'd never touch a fish, not even a little teeny pout, if you did not give it him. I was obligated to take him out a-fishing, for else he would stand and youl and marr till I went back and catched him by the pol and shied him into the boat, and then he was quite happy. When it was fire he used to stick up at the bows of the boat and sit a-watching the dogs (*i. e.* dog-fish). The dogs used to come alongside by thousands at a time, and when they was thick all about he would dive in and fetch them out, jammed in his mouth as fast as may be, just as if they was a parcel of rats, and he did not tremble with the cold half as much as a Newfoundland dog; he was used to it. He looked terrible wild about the head when he came up out of the water with the dog-fish. I larnt him the water myself. One day, when he was a kitten, I took him down to the sea to wash and brush the fleas out of him, and in a week he could swim after a feather or a cork.'

I

Of the cat in a state of nature few of us have seen very much. The wild cat has become rare in the British islands, but the specimens shot occasionally by game-keepers are very superior in size and strength to the familiar occupant of the hearth-rug. I remember that when I lived at Loch Awe, my next neighbour, a keeper on the Cladich estate, shot one that quite astonished me—a formidable beast indeed, to which the largest domestic cat was as an ordinary human being to Chang the giant—indeed this comparison is insufficient. Wild cats are not usually dangerous to man, for they prudently avoid him, but if such a creature as that killed on Lochaweside were to show fight, an unarmed man would find the situation very perilous. I would much rather have to fight a wolf. There is a tradition at the village of Barnborough, in Yorkshire, that a man and a wild cat fought together in a wood near there, and that the combat went on till they got to the church-porch, when both died from their wounds. It is the marvellous agility of the cat which makes him such a terrible enemy; to say that he 'flies' at you is scarcely a figure of speech. However, the wild cat, when he knows that he is observed, generally seeks refuge, as King Charles did at Boscobel, in the leafy shelter of some shadowy tree, and there the deadly leaden hail too surely follows him, and brings him to earth again.

Cats have the advantage of being very highly connected, since the king of beasts is their blood-relation, and it is certain that a good deal of the interest we take in them is due to this august relationship. What the merlin or the sparrow-hawk is to the golden eagle, the cat is to the great felines of the tropics. The difference between a domestic cat and a tiger is scarcely wider than that which separates a miniature pet dog from a bloodhound. It is becoming to the dignity of an African prince, like Theodore of Abyssinia, to have lions for his household pets. The true grandeur and majesty of a brave man are rarely seen in such visible supremacy as when he sits surrounded by these terrible creatures, he in his fearlessness, they in their awe; he in his defenceless weakness, they with that mighty strength which they dare not use against him. One of my friends, distinguished alike in literature and science, but not at all the sort of person, apparently, to command respect from brutes who cannot estimate intellectual greatness, had one day an interesting converation with a lion-tamer, which ended in a still more interesting experiment. The lion-tamer affirmed that there was no secret in his profession, that *real* courage alone was necessary, and that any one who had the genuine gift of courage could safely enter the cage along with him. 'For example, you yourself, sir,' added the lion-tamer, 'if you have the sort of courage I mean, may go into the cage with me whenever you like.' On this my friend, who has a fine intellectual coolness and unbounded scientific curiosity, willingly accepted the offer, and paid a visit to their majesties the lions in the privacy of their own apartment. They received him with the politeness due to a brave man, and after an agreeable interview of several minutes he backed out of the royal presence with the gratified feelings of a gentleman who has just been presented at court.

CHAPTER IV.

HORSES.

IT happened to me one night during the late war in France to ride into the court-yard of an inn which was full of French artillerymen. In the bustle and hurry of the time it was useless to call for the services of an ostler, so I set about seeking for stable-room myself. In the French country inns there are no stalls, and the only division between the horses, when there is any separation at all, is a board suspended at one end by an iron hook to the manger, and at the other hanging from the roof by a knotted cord. In this inn, however, even the hanging-board was wanting, and about fifty artillery horses were huddled together so closely as almost to touch each other, so that it was difficult to find an open space for my mare. At last I found an opening near a magnificent black animal, which I supposed to be an officer's saddle-horse.

A fine horse is always an attraction for me, so as soon as I had finished such arrangements as were possible for the comfort of my own beast, I began to examine her neighbour rather minutely. He seemed in perfect health, but at last I discovered a fresh wound on the near foreleg, evidently caused by the fragment of a shell. (There had been a battle at the place the day before.) Turning to an artilleryman who was standing by, I asked if the veterinary surgeon thought he could save the horse. 'No, sir, he is to be shot to-morrow morning.' This decision seemed hard, for the horse stood well, and was eating his hay tranquilly. I felt strongly tempted to beg him, and see what rest and care could accomplish.

At midnight I came back for my own mare. There was a great and terrible change in her neighbour's condition. He lay in the straw, half under her, the place was so crowded. I shall never forget his piteous cries and moans. He could not rise, and the shattered limb was causing him cruel pain. His noble head lay at my feet, and I stooped to caress it.

'So this is the reward,' I thought, 'that man gives to the best and bravest servant that he has! A long night of intolerable anguish, unrelieved by any attempt whatever to soothe or ease his pain; in the morning, the delayed charity of a rifle-bullet!' This single instance, which moved me because I had seen it, perhaps a little also because the animal was beautiful and gentle, what was it, after all, in comparison with the incalculable quantity of animal suffering which the war was causing in half the provinces of France? These reflections filled me with pain and sadness as I rode over the battle-ground in the frosty moonlight. The *dead* horses lay there still, just as they fell, and for them I felt no pity. Swift death, sudden oblivion, rest absolute, unconscious, eternal, these are not evils; but the pain of the torn flesh and the shattered bone, the long agony in hunger and cold, the anguish of the poor maimed brutes, who struggle through the last dark passages of existence, without either the pride of the soldier, the reason of the philosopher, or the hope of the Christian—that is Evil, pure and unmixed!

Like all who love animals much, I know and remember them as I know and remember men. During the war I had acquaintances amongst the officers and soldiers, and acquaintances amongst their horses likewise; and when they rode forth to battle I was pretty nearly as anxious about the animals as about the brave men who mounted them. I remember a Garibaldian sergeant, whose red shirt was frequently visible in my court-yard, a youth overflowing with life, to whom the excitement of a battle from time to time was as necessary as that of a ball is to a lively young lady. His way of riding was the nearest approach to that of an enraptured bard on Pegasus that I ever witnessed amongst the realities of the earth. My house is situated something like a tower, with views in every direction, and I used to amuse myself with watching him from the upper windows when the fit of equestrian inspiration was upon him. The red shirt flew first along the high-road, then dashed suddenly down a lane; a little later you could see it flashing scarlet along the outskirts of a distant wood; then, after a brief eclipse, it reappeared in the most unexpected places. The lad careered in this way simply for his amusement,—for the pulsation of that wild delight that his fiery nature needed. It is a fact that he did not even hold the reins. When these mad fits of equestrianism seized him, he flung the bridle on his charger's neck, threw his arms high in the air, and then made them revolve like the paddle-wheels of a steamer. He accompanied these gestures with wild Italian cries, and a double stroke of the spurs. No wonder if his horse galloped! And he *did* gallop. When the rider wanted to turn down a lane he simply gave his steed a hearty slap on the off-side of the neck,—a hint which never seemed to be misunderstood. I have witnessed a good deal of remarkable equestrianism, but never anything like that. His horse was one of the ugliest, and one of the best, that soldier ever bestrode. I have a faint recollection of seeing a child's wooden horse which so closely resembled it, that the artist must have had some such model in his mind. A great round barrel, that seemed as if it had been turned in a lathe, a broad chest, straight strong legs, very short proportionally, shoulders far forward relatively to the neck, high withers, large ugly head, with a good-tempered expression, a stump for a tail, and a rough coat of a bay quite closely resembling red hair in the human species: such were the various beauties of this war-horse. His ugliness and his honest looks gave me a sort of attachment to him; and his rider loved him dearly, and was loud in his praise. At length the regiment was ordered to Digon, and severely engaged there in the Battle of Pâques. Afterwards I saw the sergeant's red shirt again, but he rode no longer that good animal. The poor thing had had three of its four legs carried away by a cannon-ball; but its master, though in the heat of the battle, humanely ended its misery with his revolver.

These things, of course, are the every-day accidents of war, in which horses are killed by thousands; but when particular instances come under your observation, they pain you, if you really love animals. I heartily wish that horses could be dispensed with in war, and some sort of steam-engine used instead, if it were possible. In the orders given by Louis-Napoleon at the opening of the campaign of 1870, one detail seemed to me unnecessarily cruel. Orderlies were told not to hesitate to ride their horses to death (*de crever leurs montures*). It is certainly necessary on occasion, when the fate of thousands depends upon the speed of an animal, to avail ourselves of that noble quality by which it will give its last breath in devoted obedience; but soldiers are not generally so tender that they need to be encouraged in indiscriminate mercilessness. That glorious poem of Browning's would be intolerable to our humanity, were it not for the sweet touches of mercy at the end :—

> 'By Hasselt, Dirck groaned; and cried Joris, "Stay spur!
> Your Roos galloped bravely, the fault's not in her,
> We'll remember at Aix"—*for one heard the quick wheeze
> Of her chest, saw the stretched neck, and staggering knees,
> And sunk tail, and horrible heave of the flank,
> As down on her haunches she shuddered and sank.'* *

---

* For intense power of literary workmanship I know nothing in any language, that goes beyond those four lines.

So we were left galloping, Joris and I,
Past Looz and past Tongres, no cloud in the sky;
The broad sun above laughed a pitiless laugh,
'Neath our feet broke the brittle bright stubble, like chaff;
Till over by Dalhem a dome-spire sprang white,
And "Gallop," gasped Joris, "for Aix is in sight!"

"How they'll greet us!"—*and all in a moment his roan
Rolled neck and croup over, lay dead as a stone ;
And there was my Roland to bear the whole weight
Of the news which alone could save Aix from her fate,
With his nostrils like pits full of blood to the brim,
And with circles of red for his eye-sockets' rim.*'

All this is very terrible, and would be almost in the spirit of the Imperial command to the orderlies to *crever leurs montures ;* were it not that the very strength of the description shows how much the poet felt for the suffering animals, though he expresses no sympathy directly. But the tenderness of the man capable of loving a good horse is reserved entirely for the last two stanzas, where it is expressed in the manliest way, yet in a way so affecting that no noble-minded person who read the poem aloud could get through those last stanzas, when he came to them, without some huskiness of emotion in the voice, and, perhaps, just a little mistiness in the eyes.

' Then I cast loose my *buff coat, each holster let fall,
Shook off my jack-boots, let go belt and all,
Stood up in the stirrup, leaned, patted his ear,
Called my Roland his pet-name, my horse without peer;*
Clapped my hands, laughed and sang, any noise, bad or good,
Till at length into Aix Roland galloped and stood.

And all I remember is, friends flocking round,
And I sat with his head 'twixt my knees, on the ground;
And no voice but was praising this Roland of mine,
As I poured down his throat our last measure of wine,
Which (the burgesses voted by common consent)
Was no more than his due who brought good news from Ghent.'

This is the ideal of the relation between man and horse,—the horse serving man to his utmost, lending him his swiftness with a perfect good will,—the man accepting the service for a noble purpose, doing all he can to make the work lighter for his servant, and at last, when the great effort is over, caring for him as tenderly and anxiously as if he were a brother or a son. This is the ideal, but the reality too often falls short of it on both sides. There does not exist in the minds of owners of horses generally that touch of romantic sentiment which translates itself in affectionate companionship and tender care. The horse is a valuable animal, and is, on the whole, looked after fairly well, his health is cared for, he is usually well fed, and horses used for private purposes are seldom overworked. But there is a remarkable absence of sentiment in all this, which is proved by the facility with which, in most European countries, men sell their horses, often for bodily infirmities or imperfections, in which there is no question of temper, and especially by the custom of selling a horse which has done faithful service, merely because he is getting old and weaker than when in his prime. This last custom proves the absence of sentiment, the more completely that every one knows when selling an old horse that he is dooming him to harder work and worse keep, and that the certain fate of a horse which we part with because he is old, is a descent to harder and harder conditions, till finally he is worked to death in a cab, or in a cart belonging to some master little less miserable than himself.

The whole subject of the relation between the horse and his master depends upon the customs which regulate our life, and which have regulated the lives of our forefathers, in all sorts of other ways. We are not enough with our horses to educate either their intelligence or their affections; and as there has been the same separation in preceding centuries, the horse has inherited a way of regarding men which scarcely tends to make their relation more intimate. There are a few exceptional cases in which traces of affection are distinctly perceptible in horses, but by far the greater number of them are either indifferent, or decidedly hostile to humanity. Man loves the horse, at least some men love him, from feelings of gratitude and pride. When your horse has carried you well in battle, or on the hunting-field, you are grateful to him for the exercise of his strength and courage in your service; when he has borne you majestically on some occasion of state, or enabled you to display the grace, and skill, and the manly beauty of your person, before the admiring eyes of ladies, you are proud of him as a statue, if it could feel, would be proud of the magnificence of its pedestal. The saddle is a sort of throne for man: when seated there, he has under him the noblest of all the brutes, so that he may be said to sit enthroned above the whole animal creation. It is from a feeling of the royalty of that position, that kings, if they are good riders, always prefer to enter a city on horseback, when a great effect is to be produced upon the minds of the people, well knowing that a leathern saddle, simple and hard as it is, has more of royal dignity than the silken cushions of the gilded coach of state. An incident occurred lately on the entry of King Amadeus into Lerida, which showed him, as by an acted simile, in the character of a sovereign whose throne is not stable, yet whose hand is firm. A shower of flowers rained from a triumphal arch as the Savoyard king rode under it, and his charger plunged so violently that no one but a thorough horseman could have kept his place. All the peoples of the earth like their kings to be fine horsemen, and the crowd thought that in his tossing saddle Amadeus came royally into Lerida!

Our pride in horses, our admiration of their beauty and their strength, produce in us a certain feeling of attachment to them, but rarely a deep affection. The trouble of attending to the wants of horses, of grooming and feeding them at stated times, can rarely be undertaken by the owner himself, and would be a perpetual annoyance to him unless he had a most exceptional liking for the animal, so as to be always happy when about the stable, as schoolboys are when the first ardent φιλιππία is upon them. It is a trouble to most men to be even obliged to exercise a horse quite regularly, a rich man likes to have horses at his door when he wants them, but to have no trouble about them at other times, using them as living velocipedes, and thinking no more about them in the intervals than if they were made of well-painted iron. Hence, there comes a personage between the horse and his master, who feeds, cleans, gently exercises the animal, and is seen and heard more frequently by him in the course of one week than his owner is in a month. There are the long absences of the owner also, when he is staying in other people's houses, or travelling, or at another residence of his where he has other horses, or in his yacht where all horses whatever would be much out of place. The owner, then, from the horse's point of view, is a man who makes his appearance from time to time armed with a whip and a pair of spurs, gets upon the horse's back, compels him to trot, and gallop, and jump hedges, and then suddenly disappears, it may be for several weeks. The two lives are so widely separated that there hardly can be any warm affection. If the horse loves any one it is more likely to be the groom than the master, but the groom has often disagreeable manners (to which horses are extremely sensitive), and in some houses he is changed as frequently as a French minister. On the whole, the horse very seldom enjoys fair opportunities for attaching himself to any human being. It would be interesting for a true φίλιπποτρόφος, a rich bachelor (a wife would object to the scheme), to live permanently in a large hall, into which three or four horses of a race already intelligent should be admitted at all hours, from the time they were foals, just as dogs are in a bachelor's room in the country. They should not be tied up, but freely allowed to walk about under penalty of a reprimand if they upset the furniture, and to poke their noses over their master's shoulder when he was reading or eating his dinner, during which they should have a lettuce, or a cabbage, or something else to suit their tastes. In a word, I am supposing that in this hippic Utopia the horses should be treated as nearly as possible like dogs. It would be highly interesting to watch the effect of such a continual association between the horse and his master, and still more interesting if it could be kept up during several generations. The powers of affection in the horse are for the most part latent. We see faint signs of them, and there is a general belief that the horse has such powers, which is founded partly on some exceptional examples, and partly on a subtle satisfaction in believing that we are beloved by our slaves. But the plain truth is, that horses, as they live usually in our service, have little to love us for, and most commonly regard us either with indifference or dislike. The slightest demonstration of attachment wins us in a moment, and we exaggerate it because it flatters our *amour propre*. When a horse neighs at our coming, it is most commonly a request for corn, and some of his other demonstrations are very equivocal. Some men tell you when their horses set their ears back, and show the white of their eye, and try to bite, and kick at them in the stable, that all these are merely signs of playful affection. In short, there is a distinct passion in man's heart for which the Greeks had a name, but which in England we call the love of horses, and this has its illusions like every other passion. Knowing this, I hardly dare venture to say precisely what I think about the horse, but a well-known French saying is applicable to his case: *En amour, l'un des deux aime, et l'autre se laisse aimer.* So I should say of the horse, *il se laisse aimer.*

When we come to the active vices, the hatred and rebellion of the horse against his master express themselves very plainly, much more plainly than equine affection expresses itself ever. Many of these vices are hereditary in the equine blood, are a tradition of ill-usage. The way in which they burst forth in horses, apparently of the most tranquil character, is one of the mysteries of nature. Three instances have occurred in my own stable, of animals becoming suddenly and irremediably vicious, passing in the course of three or four days from a state like that of Paris under the Empire to the rage and rebellion of Paris under the Commune, and neither in these cases, nor in any other that has come under my observation, has a *real vice* ever been permanently eradicated. Horses become vicious from many causes; the most frequent, I think, is idleness, in combination with confinement and good keep. Out at grass a horse becomes wild rather than vicious, and mere wildness is easily curable by gentleness and patience. Tied up in a stable, with plenty of hay and corn, his system accumulates the electricity of irritability which ought to have been regularly expanded in work, and it explodes in dangerous violence. Four days' idleness in an inn-stable, during wet weather, cost me the most valuable horse I ever possessed. On the fifth day no man could ride him, and no man was ever able to ride him afterwards.* A black Irish horse, who served me well during a year, and was an excellent leaper, was suddenly lost to me in the same way, and the same thing occurred with a powerful Scotch Galloway. Most men who have had some experience of horses will have known such cases. No form of disappointment is more provoking. The animal, after vice has declared itself, seems exactly the same creature that he did before. Has he not the same limbs, shape, colour? Is not the spot of white upon his forehead precisely in the same place? Is not his tail of the same length? Nothing is altered that the eye may detect, but there is the same change that there is in a wine-bottle when somebody has poured the wine out and replaced it with deadly poison. In the animal's brain there dwelt a spirit that was your most faithful servant—your most humble and dutiful friend; that spirit is gone, and instead of it there is a demon who is determined to kill you whenever an opportunity offers. The Teutonic legends of black steeds with fiery eyes that

* I begged the late Lord Hawke, who was the best rider, or one of the three best, I ever knew, to make a trial of him, but the results were the same as with myself and the rough-riders, and the verdict, "Nothing to be made of him."

K

were possessed by evil spirits, are no more than the poetical form that clothes an indubitable truth. The nature of the horse is such that he is capable of endless irreconcilable rage, against his master, and against humanity,—a temper of chronic hate and rebellion like that of Milton's fallen angels, keeping the fierce resolve—

> 'To wage by force or guile eternal war
> Irreconcilable.'

If there is anything in the world of nature that seems clear, morally, it is, that man has an authentic right to require reasonable service from the horse. The adaptation of the animal to labour of various kinds, the use that man has made of him from the dawn of history, are enough to prove a Divine intention. It is foolish enough, I know, to carry speculation about Divine intentions far, because slave-owners might speak, and have spoken, of obvious Divine intentions in their favour; and if a tiger ever wasted his time in theological controversy, he might prove a Divine intention in favour of his eating Englishmen. However this may be, I feel perfectly satisfied that man was made to be equestrian (at least, a certain proportion of mankind), and that the horse was made to carry him; and with this conviction I have no hesitation in making the horse do his duty, by gentle means, if possible,—by harsher means, if necessary. But when a horse is once really and truly possessed by a devil, gentleness is of no use. Then come the great combats, the great cruelties; and the more cruel you are the more does the creature hate you. If you are mild, he regards you with contempt; if harsh, with ever-increasing hatred. In these cases there is no medium, and it is only men who are endowed with a peculiar physical (perhaps magnetic) influence over horses, who can effect anything like a reconciliation.

When you see, however, the thousands upon thousands of horses which do their duty, on the whole safely and well, in London, in the country, in the army, about railway-stations, breweries, and business places of all kinds, you will conclude that the horse-demons are rare in proportion; and, indeed, happily they are so. Most horses are fairly good, and in some races almost all of them are docile. In other races vices of different kinds are very common. Take the Corsican ponies, for instance, a hardy little race of much speed and endurance, very useful to drive in pairs in small phaetons; they are nearly always vicious, though seldom vicious enough to interfere materially with their usefulness. A tiny pair were offered me with a pretty carriage, the whole equipage suspiciously cheap, but I discovered that one of the charming little creatures would kick like the youthful Tommy Newcome in Doyle's sketch, and the other bit like a wolf. Afterwards, I found that these accomplishments were common to the Corsican breed; in fact, that they were generally as energetic, but as wilful and difficult to deal with, as their little human compatriot, Napoleon. On the other hand, there are breeds where gentle tempers and amiable manners are hereditary.

In the etchings which accompany this chapter, Veyrassat has given us the horse at liberty and in service. Both plates represent very happy moments of equine life, for sweet to the horse are the Elysian fields of liberty, and sweet also the hour of rest, and the feed by the wayside inn.

CHAPTER V.

HORSES (*continued*).

THE second of the two illustrations which accompany this chapter, representing horses on a battle-field, has none of the romantic beauty with which painters have so often given a delusive charm to subjects of a like nature; but the ugliness of this etching (a sort of ugliness which is quite admissible in serious art) may be attributed to strong and recent impressions received by the artist from the reality itself. The peaceful inhabitants of London have ideas about cavalry horses which would be greatly modified by a week's experience of Continental warfare. The British army requires few horses in comparison with the vast numbers which are absorbed by the forces of Germany or France, so that there is wider latitude for selection, and no horse which has the honour of carrying a British soldier is ever publicly seen in his native land without having everything that can affect his appearance entirely in his favour. The man who rides him, though apparently his master, is in reality his servant, as every youth who enters the ranks of a cavalry regiment discovers when his young illusions fade. All the things which the animal has to carry are, by the craft and taste of the clever equipment-makers, turned into so many ornaments; and even when not positively beautiful in themselves, are so devised as to enhance the martial effect, and make you feel that you are in the presence of a war-horse. Bright steel and brass, in forms unused about the saddlery of civilians; furs and saddle-cloths, the latter decorated with lace round the edges, and perhaps even embroidery in the corners; a luxury of straps and chains, a massiveness peculiarly military; all this strikes the civilian imagination, and the battle-steed, even when not in himself a particularly perfect animal, has generally a noble and imposing air. All his belongings are kept so clean and bright that we respect him as a member of the aristocracy of horses. He is brushed and groomed as if he came from the stables of a prince. To these advantages may be added that of his superior education, which tells in every movement, and his pride, for he is proud of all his superiorities, and the consciousness of them gives grace to the curve of his neck, and fire to his eye, and dignity to his disdainful stepping.

These glories of the war-horse are to be seen in their highest perfection in that prosperous and peaceful capital of England where the thunder of an enemy's cannon has never yet been heard. The English household troops are the ideal cavalry, good in service on the field of serious conflict, but especially and peculiarly admirable as a spectacle. I had almost written that the poetry of warfare was to be best seen in a charge of the Life-guards at a review, but there is a yet deeper poetry in some of war's realities where the element of beauty is not so conspicuously present. The boy's ideal of the war-horse is that coal-black, silken coated charger that bears the helmeted cuirassier, and all those glittering arms and ornaments dazzle the imagination and fill the martial dreams of youth. Well, it is very fine, very beautiful, and we like to see the Royal Guards flashing past after the Court carriages; but last winter I saw another sight, and renounced the boy's ideal.

The armies of Chanzy had been defeated on the Loire, and their broken remnants passed as they could to join the desperate enterprise of Bourbaki for the relief of Belfort. In the depth of that terrible winter, the roads covered with snow, with a bitter wind sweeping across the country from the east, and every water-fall a pillar of massy ice, there came two or three thousand horsemen from those disastrous battle-fields. Slowly they passed over the hills that divide the eastern from the western rivers, an irregular procession broken by great intervals, so that we always thought no more of them were coming, yet others followed, straggling in melancholy groups. What a contrast to the brilliance of a review! How different from the marchings-past when the Emperor sat in his embroidery on the Champ-de-Mars and the glittering hosts swept before him, saluting with polished swords! Ah, these horsemen came from another and a bloodier field of Mars; they had been doing the rough work of the war-god and bore the signs of it! The brass of their helmets shone no more than the dull leopard-skin beneath it, the lancers had poles without pennons, the bits and stirrups were rusty, and the horses were encumbered with tins and pans for rude cookery, and bundles of hay, and coarse coverings for the bitter bivouac. Here and there a wearied brute was led slowly by a merciful master; a few were still suffering from wounds, all were meagre and overworked, not one had been groomed for weeks. Yet here, I said, as the weary troops passed by, and others like them loomed in grey masses as they approached through the falling snow,—here, and not on the brilliant parade-ground, now in this busy harvest-time of death, not then in the lightness of their leisure, are the battle-steeds most sublime! All the fopperies of soldiering had been rubbed away by the rough hand of implacable Necessity, but instead of them what a moving pathos! what grandeur of patient endurance! Grotesque they all were certainly, but it was a grotesqueness of that highest kind which is infinitely and irresistibly affecting. The women laughed at those sorry brutes, those meagre Rosinantes, and at the wonderful odd figures that sat upon them, like Quixotes in quilts, riding on the wildest of expeditions to meet starvation under the dark Jura pine-trees,—but whilst the women laughed the tears ran down their cheeks. And here, in this etching of Veyrassat, you see what the poor creatures were going to, and how at last they were permitted to take their rest. Yes, here you have the plain truth about the war-horse. Veyrassat has not represented him as a delicately-bred animal, and he has treated his saddlery with the most complete indifference. This comes of having been recently impressed by a sight of the reality. Artists who have never seen war are usually very particular about spots of light on stirrup and bit, and about the various inventions of the military clothier, but Veyrassat has told his tale very plainly by the expression of the two heads and bodies, the dead horse lying like, what he is, a mere heap of unconscious carrion, the wounded one vainly endeavouring to rise and neighing to his departing friends which he will accompany no more. Horses feel these separations more than they feel any separation from human friend or master, so that this is a touch of nature. A dog would have been occupied in passionate outbreaks of lamentation for his master lying stretched there on the turf, and would have neither followed, nor thought of following, any living being; but the horse forms his friendships amongst creatures of his own kind. Not to be able to go along with his old comrades, to be fixed to one spot of turf by a shattered limb whilst they are galloping to the horizon, must be the most cruel pain that this creature can ever suffer in his sentiments and affections.

The conspicuous merit of the horse, which has given him the dearly-paid honour of sharing in our wars, is his capacity for being disciplined,—and a very great capacity it is, a very noble gift indeed; nobler than much cleverness. Several animals are cleverer than the horse in the way of intelligence; not one is so amenable to discipline. He is not observant, except of places; not nearly so observant as half-a-dozen other animals we know. His eye never fixes itself long in a penetrating gaze, like the mild, wistful watchfulness of the dog, or the steady flame of the lion's luminous orbs, but he can listen and obey, and his acts of obedience pass easily by repetition into fixed habits, so that you never have to teach him more than one thing at a time. The way to educate a horse is to do as Franklin did in the formation of his moral habits—that is, to aim at one perfection at once, and afterwards, when that has become easy from practice, and formed itself into a habit, to try for some other perfection. A good horse never forgets your lessons. There are unteachable brutes which ought to be handed over to rude masters and rough work, but every horse of average intelligence and gentle temper may be very highly educated indeed. Beyond this average degree of teachableness there are exceptional cases—the horses of genius; for genius (an exceptional vigour and intensity of the mental faculties with correspondingly larger powers of acquisition) exists amongst the lower animals in due degree as it does in the human species. A few animals of this remarkable degree of endowment are picked up by the proprietors of circuses, and so become known to the public, but the probability is that a much larger proportion remain in the obscurity of ordinary equine life, and that their gifts escape attention. Most of us have seen remarkable performances of trained horses. The most remarkable that I ever saw were those of that wonderful black gelding that Pablo Fanque used to ride. There can be no doubt that he had pride and delight in his own extraordinary intelligence and perfect education, just as some great poet or painter may delight in the richness of his gifts and the perfection of his work. But the circus performance is not the ideal aim of equine accomplishment. One would not care much to have a horse that would dance or fire a pistol, or pick up a pocket-handkerchief, yet it would be pleasant to have in our horses the degree of docility and intelligence which circus-trainers direct to these vain objects. Many accomplishments might be attained that would be valuable everywhere. It would be extremely convenient if a horse would follow you without being pulled by halter or bridle, and wait for you in one place without being fastened. A man who had travelled amongst the Arabs told me that he had seen many horses that would stand where they were left, without any fastening, and some will follow you like a dog. A great deal of accomplishment may go into the ordinary work of saddle and carriage-horses, and almost escape notice because we think it only natural. But how wide is the difference between a trained horse and a raw one! How slight are the indications by which the master conveys the expression of his will, how rapid and exact the apprehension! With horses of the finest organisation this apprehension rises into a sympathy above the necessity for any definite command, they know the master's will by a sense of faint pressures, of limb on saddle, of hand on rein. I used to ride a horse which would go on trotting so long as I was not tired, but when I began to feel fatigued he walked, knowing by my altered manner of rising in the saddle that rest would be a relief to me. By this accurate interpretation of our muscular action, even when it is so slight as to be imperceptible to the eye of a by-stander, the horse measures the skill, the strength, the resolution of his rider. He knows at once whether you are at home in the saddle or not, and if your movements do not correspond accurately to his own, he is aware that he can take liberties. A bad rider may sometimes deceive the people in the street, but it may be doubted whether he ever deceived the animal under him. It is evident that a bad rider must be extremely disagreeable to a horse of refined feeling, disagreeable as an awkward partner in dancing is disagreeable. The intelligence of horses is shown in nothing so much as in their different behaviour under different men. When a thorough horseman gets into the saddle the creature he mounts is aware that there are the strongest reasons for behaving himself properly, and it is only the mad rebels that resist. Not only can a good horseman overcome opposition better than a bad one, but he has much less opposition to overcome. The very best horsemen, amongst gentlemen, are often scarcely even aware of the real difficulties of riding, their horses obey them so well, and are so perfectly suited to their work. An English lady who rides admirably, told me that she did not deserve so much credit as she got, because the excellence of her horses made riding quite easy for her, and she declared that even in her boldest leaps the *secousse* was not very violent. There is a good deal of truth in this, which is often overlooked. The relation between horse and rider is mutual, and each shows the other to advantage.

Whilst on this subject of riding, let me express a regret that good horsemanship is becoming rarer and rarer in proportion to the numbers of the population. The excellence of modern roads, which has led to the universal employment of wheeled carriages, and the introduction of railways, which are now used by all classes for long or rapid journeys, have together reduced horsemanship, in the case of civilians, to the rank of a mere amusement, or an exercise for the benefit of health. In fact, it is coming to this, that nobody but rich men and their grooms will know how to ride on horseback; whereas in former generations, when the bad roads reduced all travelling to an alternative between riding and pedestrianism, men of all degrees and conditions went on horseback for considerable distances, and became skilful, no doubt, in proportion to the frequency of their practice. What a great deal of riding there is in the Waverley novels! Not only the baron and the knight, but also the tradesman, the commercial traveller, the citizen of every rank, go on horseback from place to place. How much healthy and invigorating exercise the men of our generation miss which their forefathers frequently enjoyed! Imagine the benefit to a manly youth of the last century, fastened in

London behind a counter or a desk, when he was ordered to ride on business to Lincoln, or York, or Edinburgh! He had before him weeks of the manliest life a human being can lead, and plenty of leisure, as he sat in the saddle, for the observation of men and nature. There was danger enough to give exercise to his courage; and as the pistols in his holsters were loaded with powder and ball, so the heart in his breast had to be charged with the spirit of the brave. All men in those days lived from time to time a life giving them some brotherhood with the knights of the days of chivalry. A London tradesman riding over the dark heath, robber-haunted, thinking about the flints of his big pistols, had need of a portion of that manliness which in other times had clothed itself in knightly harness of complete steel. Consider the difference between passing a fortnight on horseback and a night in a railway train—the long breathing of fresh air, the healthy exercise, the delightful variety of scenery, the entertaining change and adventure; and then the seat in the corner of a railway carriage, with a poisonously impure atmosphere, and a hot-water tin under your feet! Whoever heard of an equestrian wanting a hot-water tin? An ingenious French saddler invented stirrups with lanterns under them for night-travelling, and the lanterns heated small foot-warmers, but his invention had no sale. On the other hand, you really cannot do without a foot-warmer in a carriage when the thermometer is below freezing-point. This marks the difference of the two as to exercise. Railway travelling is fatiguing, yet it is not exercise. It wears the nervous system, but does not help the circulation of the blood. Horse exercise produces effects of an exactly opposite nature, it stimulates and improves the circulation, and reposes the nervous system better than anything except swimming. Our forefathers found in travel a double corrective for the evils of a sedentary life, and they had the additional advantage of not being able to go far without spending a good deal of time upon the road—days and weeks— during which the system had full leisure to recruit itself. Too many of them were senselessly careless about health; they ate and drank a great deal more than can have been good for them, and the more robust had little notion of moderation in anything: yet they certainly knew less of nervous ailments than does our own more thoughtful and scientific generation. Their bad roads gave them exercise, as their badly-fitted doors and windows ensured them an efficient ventilation. We may still imitate them in equestrian tours; but it is not quite the same thing, because we only travel in this way for pleasure, that is, when we take a holiday, whereas they did it from necessity, at all seasons and in all weathers.

I read the other day, in a book written for students, that walking, and not riding, is the best exercise; and I knew a physician who said he only recommended horse exercise because his patients preferred it. On this point it may be observed, that no one is likely to get much good in the saddle unless he has the true equestrian instinct, which is as much a gift of nature as the love of aquatics. Without the natural instinct you cannot feel the peculiar exhilaration which gladdens the born horseman and relieves him from that burden of his cares. There is an exulting sense of augmented power in the breast of such a man when he feels that all the strength and swiftness of the noble animal that bears him have become his own swiftness and his own strength ; that he, who but a moment before was the slowest of creatures, may now follow the wild fox and the antelope ; that, if need were, he could traverse three horizons in a day. It is this pride and delight of horsemanship, and not the mere physical exertion, which gladden the heart of man and add to his health and courage. Can any sensation be finer than that of a good rider, well mounted, going across country at full speed ? Only one other sensation is comparable to it, that of steering a lively vessel when the mainsail is wet with spray, and the sheet is straining tight, and the topmast bends like whalebone, and the wind blows fair and free !

An American newspaper lamented not long ago that rich men in the United States had such a mania for driving that they had thrown the saddle aside. The same evil may be observed in France, and is even perceptible in England, the last stronghold of noble equestrianism. The excellence of modern roads, and the perfection of modern carriage-building, have brought about this result. Thousands of men own horses in these days who never bought such a thing as a saddle, and would not know what to do if hoisted into one; and their carriages are so very luxurious as to be beneficial to nobody but invalids. There are three classes of horse-owners—the men who can ride, the men who can drive, and lastly the men who can sit still and be driven about by a coachman. To the last the horse is purely and simply a locomotive, into which his owner puts fuel and water at stated times that it may make his wheels go round. The drivers take a real interest in horses, and often show great courage and attain quite a surprising skill. Much may be said in favour of their amusement, which has a fine excitement of its own. A rider commands only one horse, a driver may hold four in his hand at once; a rider hears no sound but that of hoofs, the driver hears also the lively rumble of the wheels, and feels the pleasant springing and swinging of the well-built vehicle under him. The rider serves no one but himself, the driver has an agreeable sense of importance when the drag is crowded with fair passengers for whose safety he feels himself responsible. Our modern usages, which prohibit splendid saddlery to civilians and have made all ornamentation of it inconsistent with good taste, still allow some splendour in carriage-harness, silver crests and buckles, and other things not absolutely necessary, and in the carriages themselves there are displays of wealth and luxury which could never be concentrated in a saddle. When a rich man has a taste for ostentation, he gratifies it more easily in carriages than in saddle-horses. When a poor man has five children and one horse, the beast cannot carry the whole family on his back, but he can easily drag it behind him in a four-wheeled conveyance. Even a bachelor who keeps only one horse has cogent reasons for preferring harness. A saddle-horse can carry his own person, but his owner cannot take a servant with him nor offer a place to a friend. All the reasons of convenience (the most powerful of all reasons in the long run) are on the side of harness in every country where the roads are good. There are parts of France where it is already thought an eccentricity to ride on horseback, and where equestrians are so rare that if ever one makes his appearance the children stare and laugh, and the grown-up people smile, as they would at a man on stilts. In neighbourhoods of that kind it is dangerous to a man's reputation for gravity to be seen on horseback, and men of serious pretensions have the same objection to the saddle that a bishop has to a bicycle. Hunting and war keep up the art of riding; without them it would be in great danger of going out altogether, as falconry has gone out, to be revived, like falconry, at some future period by a few persons of wealth and leisure, as a curiosity of ancestral custom.

The influence of the turf on horses and on horsemanship deserves more thorough investigation than these brief chapters would permit. It does little or no good to riding, except by creating a special professional class with quite peculiar professional aims; and it does no good whatever to the breeding of horses, except by transmitting the capacity for great speed at a sudden 'spurt,' which is usually purchased at the cost of substantial qualities more valuable for common use. Practically, I believe, the most public benefit that the turf has given to England has been her rapid Hansoms. They are very commonly horsed, directly or indirectly, from the turf, and the swiftness which whirls you through the interminable streets of London has been first developed, either in the horse that drags you or in some ancestor of his, for the chance of a triumph at Epsom, or Newmarket, or Doncaster.

The turf, as it is followed, is not really an equestrian recreation, any more than the watching of hired gladiators was warfare. The swiftness of horses, being always various and always having elements of chance, was found to be a convenient subject for betting, and the excitement of being in a great crowd on a race course was found to be agreeable to everybody in search of a stimulus. Races are a popular institution; vacant minds like them; and they are liked also as an amusement by some minds too distinguished in serious pursuits to be liable to any accusation of vacancy. Yet it seems probable that the truest lover of horses would be of all men the least likely to devote himself passionately to the turf. What, to him, could be the pleasure of keeping animals to be trained and ridden by paid agents, and never to know their master?

The influence of the turf upon the physical perfection of the horse has not been favourable to his beauty. The race-horse has lost the beauty of nature in one direction, as the prize-pig has departed from it in another. That which his forms express is not beauty, but culture. You see at once that he is a highly artificial product, the creature of wealth and civilization. Many people admire him for that, because there is an inextricable confusion in the popular mind between ideas of beauty and ideas of careful cultivation. The race-horse has the charms of a tail-coat, of a trained pear-tree, of all such superfine results of human ingenuity, but he has lost the glory of nature. Look at his straight neck, at the way he holds his head, at his eager, anxious eye, often irritable and vicious! Breeders for the turf have succeeded in substituting the straight line for the curve, as the dominant expressional line, a sure and scientific manner of eradicating the elements of beauty. No real artist would ever paint race-horses from choice. Good artists have occasionally painted them for money. The meagre limbs, straight lines, and shiny coat, have slight charms for an artist, who generally chooses either what is beautiful or what is picturesque, and the race-horse is neither picturesque nor beautiful. Imagine what would become of the frieze of the Parthenon if you substituted modern race-horses for those admirable little chargers the Athenian loved so well! They have the true hippic beauty: fine curves everywhere: if they are not servile copies of pure nature, it is only because they reach a still higher fidelity to the Divine idea. Yet there exists a type superior even to the noble horse of Phidias. In the heart of Nejed, where the long-pursed unbeliever comes not, blooms the flower of equine loveliness. Who that delights in horses would not envy Mr. Palgrave his sight of the stables of Feysul, the royal stables of Nejed? *Ut rosa flos florum,* so are those the stables of stables! The bold traveller, at his life's hazard, saw with his bodily eyes what our painters see only in their dreams!

'Never,' he wrote afterwards, 'never had I seen or imagined so lovely a collection. Their stature was indeed somewhat low: I do not think that any came fully up to fifteen hands; fourteen appeared to me about their average; but they were so exquisitely well shaped, that want of greater size seemed hardly, if at all, a defect. Remarkably full in the haunches, with a shoulder of a slope so elegant as to make one, in the words of an Arab poet, go "raving mad about it;" a little, a very little saddle-backed, just the curve which indicates springiness without any weakness; a head, broad above, and tapering down to a nose fine enough to verify the phrase of "drinking from a pint-pot"—did pint-pots exist in Nejed; a most intelligent and yet a singularly gentle look, full eye, sharp, thorn-like little ear; legs, fore and hind, that seemed as if made of hammered iron, so clean and yet so well twisted with sinew; a neat round hoof, just the requisite for hard ground; the tail set on or rather thrown out at a perfect arch; coats smooth, shining, and light; the mane long, but not over-grown nor heavy; and an air and step that seemed to say, "Look at me, am I not pretty?"—their appearance justified all reputation, all value, all poetry. The prevailing colour was chestnut or grey, a light bay, an iron colour; white or black were less common; full bay, flea-bitten, or pie-bald, none. But if asked what are, after all, the specially distinctive points of the Nejdee horse, I should reply—the slope of the shoulder, the extreme cleanness of the shank, and the full-rounded haunch, though every other part, too, has a perfection and a harmony unwitnessed (at least by my eyes) anywhere else.'

Even the Arabs we see in Europe, however inferior to that purest breed of Nejed, are enough to make clear to us what the Arabian ideal is. That it is the central Divine conception of horse-beauty, I think no artist doubts, though artists often prefer other races from affection, or because their own art is more picturesque than beautiful. Veyrassat, for instance, who can etch cart-horses as nobody else can etch them, has never, I believe, cared to illustrate the more graceful breeds that excite the enthusiasm of poets. So it has been with Rosa Bonheur, and the whole picturesque school generally; they take naturally to the cart-horse, whose massive grandeur satisfies them. Preferences of this kind, in the practice of artists, do not, however, prove anything against the supreme beauty of the Arab. The best painters always work more from sympathy and affection than from admiration, and they take as models, not what even they themselves consider most beautiful, but what will take its place best in the class of pictures that they paint. The truth is, that the Arab is much *too* beautiful to be admissible in the pictures of the rustic schools; he would spoil everything around him, he would be as much out of place as a Greek statue in a cottage interior. Even the Greek horses of Phidias are too noble to be ridden by cavaliers not endowed with the full beauty of the human body, beautiful strong arms to hold the restraining bridle, beautiful strong legs to press the charger's sides! And how then shall you paint the daintily-exquisite Arab along with wooden-shod Normandy peasants, and fustian-breeched Yorkshire grooms? Where shall we find a rider worthy of him? Not the mean-looking modern Sultan, going cloaked to the Mosque on a Friday; not even the white-robed Emir, ringed by a host of spears! Far in the distance of the past rises the one romantic figure worthy to mount the perfect Arab. Rich in jewelled caparison, the faultless horse awaits him! The saddle is empty as yet, and its diamonds flash in the torchlight, but the little sharp ears are listening, they have detected the step of the master! There is a movement in far corridors, the golden gates are open. Like a stream that glitters in moonlight, the court descends the stair! The master sits in the saddle, the proud steed steps along the street; all men are prostrate before the Caliph.

> 'Sole star of all that place and time
> I see him---in his golden prime,
> The good Haroun Alraschid!'

CHAPTER VI.

THE BOVINES.

THE patient oxen! This is their main virtue, patience. And their chief gift or endowment is strength. No animal known to us in Western Europe has patience comparable to that of the ox, and for vast strength, steadily exerted, he is above rivalry. The dray-horse is as strong, but he does not possess the persistent steadiness of trained oxen. The bovines have not the horse's irritability; their temper is very calm, slow to anger, and of infinite endurance. They work always upon nature's grand old principle of unhurried but untiring application, pushing on always with pressure equal to their task, as if life in this world were infinite for them, and the hours, instead of flying, walked on at their own slow pace. Better servants man never had, and notwithstanding their slowness they achieve enormous results.

The animals which work for us show their character, as men do, in their work; and therefore, in speaking of the working animals, let me inquire, first, how they acquit themselves in service. The time when these animals are grandest is not, I think, their idle time; not the hours they pass in luxurious indolence at summer noontide, under the shade of widely-spreading trees, but their moments of supreme effort in harness, dragging great wains home in the late evening, when the sky is charged with thunder and the harvest is hastily garnered.

It has always seemed inexplicable to me that oxen should be so much used for labour in one country and not used at all in another not divided from it by any visible line of demarcation, and that this usage of employing oxen in agriculture should descend traditionally in some places and not spread itself in other places where there seems to be no reason for believing that they would not be equally useful. I can only suggest, as a possible explanation, that in some regions the breeds are better adapted for labour than they are in others; though, of course, there would be the obvious answer, that when people really care to possess any kind of animal that can be easily acclimatised in their land, they take the trouble to import it. I imagine that, for agriculture of a primitive kind, such as that common in the regions where oxen are principally used, the advantages of employing these animals or horses are so very nearly and nicely balanced, that mere habit and tradition will settle the question either way; but it is clear that, to very small farmers indeed, such as the poor peasant landowners of France, there is a gain in employing oxen or cows, because they are sure to have some animals of that kind, whereas a horse is as much a matter of separate acquisition as a steam-engine. It is very possible that prejudice may interfere in this matter as it does in so many others, even against pecuniary interest; and just as Europeans have been in the habit of throwing away an incalculable number of tons of excellent animal food, because they had a traditional prejudice against horse-flesh, so, on the other hand, may they have gone on rejecting an incalculable amount of valuable service because they had a traditional idea that oxen were not intended for the yoke. They are used in some out-of-the-way corners in England, but I have never seen them used there, and it is possible that most of our English breeds may be too refined and delicate to be efficient in farm-labour; they are sometimes exquisite in form, but are not always massive enough in the skeleton for very heavy work. In countries, however, where oxen are commonly employed, there is little hesitation about using rather delicate animals; more of them are yoked, and the necessary amount of force is obtained. The difference of custom in the employment of oxen cannot be seen in a more striking manner than by visiting two old French cities, Sens and Autun, each on a market-day. Of the fifteen hundred vehicles that go to the market at Sens, not one is drawn by oxen; or if there should be one, it is a chance which may happen twice in a twelvemonth. At Autun, on the contrary, you will find perhaps a thousand pairs, all the heavy work being given to oxen in that neighbourhood, whilst the light work, requiring speed, is reserved for horses. But the line of demarcation may be fixed more accurately than that. In Eastern France that line is the vine-covered slope of the Côte d'Or. To the west of it oxen are used constantly; to the east of it they are used little or not at all. I have never been able to discover any reason for this except a traditional custom. The oxen are in this case used in a poorer, and the horses in a richer district; but it would be unsafe to draw any general inference from that, as it happens sometimes that a comparatively wealthy country will use oxen, whilst a poorer one will be as faithful to horses as are the inhabitants of gold-accumulating Manchester or Middlesex.

These animals, though not of quick intelligence, are very easily educated. To break in one of them the farmer simply takes and yokes him with one which has seen a year or two of service. The novice requires special attention during the first day or two, but he gradually gets accustomed to his duty, and comes to understand the various signs and sounds by which the will of his master is communicated to him. As his temper is usually equable, it is not so much any active vice that has to be overcome as a certain slowness of understanding. I had almost written 'stupidity,' but that would be scarcely just. The ox is not really stupid, but he has Saxon slowness, which is a different thing. When a pair of oxen are to be educated *together*, as it is sometimes desirable that they should be, they are placed in a team of six, with a thoroughly trained pair before them and another in their rear. At first they get dragged by those in front, or tormented by the horns of those behind, but in a few days they work steadily enough to be tried in a cart or waggon by themselves. No doubt the manner of ruling them varies in different countries, that which I know consists of a certain series of motions with the goad, including frequent encouragements with the voice. To direct a pair of oxen is something like rowing a boat, and requires, in its way, as much skill and science. I mean, that in using the goad you must know the exact effect it will have upon the animal's motions, which at first is not by any means easy. A gentleman unaccustomed to this kind of driving could no more take a pair of oxen through a crowd of vehicles than a peasant could take an outrigger from Twickenham to Kew. If you lay the wand gently between the horns of one of your oxen, he will follow you, but unless you very soon do as much for the other your waggon will begin to turn, because the other will think it his duty to hang back. If you want to turn rapidly, you strike the inner ox across the face with the wand (as gently as you like, it is a mere conventional sign between you and him), and laying your wand between the horns of the outer ox make him follow you. If both are to back (and you can make them back a considerable distance), you strike both across the face repeatedly and somewhat sharply. The peasants of the Morvan and the Nivernais always call their oxen by special names, and as the beasts know their names as well as dogs do, this saves much use of the goad. A man will drive a team of six almost entirely by the voice, calling to each animal by his name, when it does not take its full share of the work, or in any other way needs a word of admonition. I need not go more deeply into the system of signs by which the goad is made to convey so much to the bovine mind, as it is scarcely probable that the reader will ever practically require any knowledge of this kind; but it may be observed generally, that pricking an ox in one part of his body and pricking him in another do not by any means produce the same consequences. It is a system of signs, a language, which the ox perfectly understands, and if you use it without understanding it you will produce unforeseen, and possibly disastrous effects, like a traveller in a foreign land who gives orders in words whose significance he has not thoroughly mastered.

When the day's work is at an end and the wearied teams come back to the stable, it is a pretty sight to see them standing in pairs together, still yoked, though detached from the waggon or the plough. In a farm where the oxen are properly disciplined, each pair will wait in their place until the farmer, who stands at the door of the stable, calls for them in their turn. Then they march forward to the stable-door and bow their mighty necks to his hand, that he may remove the yoke; and when the last thong is unwound, and the straw cushions and wooden arches are taken away, they lift up their free heads gladly, and each one goes to his place. Prettier still is their perfect submission when the yoke is put on in the morning, often by some little boy scarcely emerged from childhood, whom yet they obey with an elephantine meekness. When we consider how frequently oxen are changed, it is surprising that accidents should be so rare.

It is inevitable that there should be a wide difference of opinion between artists and scientific breeders concerning the beauty of the bovine races. Indeed, there is a confusion in the employment of the mere word, by people who do not mean the same thing by it. If you breed cattle with a view to the dairy or the butcher, you come to regard them mainly as either cheese-and-butter-producing animals or else beef-producing animals, and then a process begins to operate in your mind, to which all human minds are so subject that the wisest of them cannot escape it—the process of perversion of judgment on one matter by association of ideas with another matter. You come to tolerate, and more than tolerate, even to approve and admire, those peculiarities of form which are associated with the kind of productiveness you wish for, till finally you arrive at those ideas of beauty which prevail in the engravings on inn-walls in very advanced agricultural counties and at the great agricultural shows. In places where oxen are constantly used for labour there is less danger of this, because if they are to have fine working qualities they must have good natural shape—a strong bony structure, to begin with, well-developed muscles, and little superfluous fat. The difference between an animal of this kind and an ox bred for beef is very like the difference between an active young Englishman and Daniel Lambert, who may be still remembered by some readers as the fattest man of his generation. It is unnecessary to dwell long upon this difference when it is so strikingly marked as it is in the case of the animals which win prizes, because every reader having artistic tastes (and one who had not would not read an essay of this kind) sees at a glance that such animals have lost all natural beauty, and gained in exchange for it nothing but an increased value as material for the food-market. The real danger in this and many other things like it, most peculiarly and especially to people living in England, is an insensible perversion or vitiation of sound natural taste by the continual sight of types which are not monstrous enough to strike the eye as monstrosities, but are half-way between Nature and the consummated triumph of the cattle-breeder. England is an intensely artificial country in all those parts of it which are cultivated at all, and culture of all kinds is carried so very far, always in the direction of material increase, that it is difficult to get to see genuine nature there, either in landscape or animal beauty.* In a word, it is a large garden, and as botanists tell us that we ought not to study botany in gardens, so it is unwise to study animal form where it has been developed on the principles of the gardener.

I said that our artificial breeds had lost all natural

* Readers who happen to be exceptionally placed may demur to this, but it is strictly true of the majority of English counties. The advance of scientific agriculture is the death of artistic interest. After a railway journey through England Rosa Bonheur said, ' *Vous avez tué le pittoresque.*' We have done more, we have killed the *beautiful* also.

beauty, not having space just then to make the necessary reserves. But there is an important natural law with reference to human interference which cannot be overlooked. The law is this. Man may destroy beauty of form in living plants and animals, but he cannot destroy all those minor beauties of texture and surface in which nature often in some measure seeks a compensation for the absence of nobler perfections. The prize cow is as to shape merely a collection of deformities; but Nature gives her hide a beautiful texture, and her eyes are like dark jewels, only better rounded and polished than jewel ever was. So, though I have just written that we in England have killed, not only the picturesque, as Rosa Bonheur said we had done, but the beautiful also;—I meant that noble form of the beautiful which rules the main lines of things when Nature has her way: the grand slopes of far-stretching landscape, unbroken by wall or fence, the tufted distances of boundless forest, and the free curves of the unimpeded stream. Yet there still remains, even in the trimly-fenced pasture where the sleek beeves are feeding, some beauty of surface, like the beauty of their own hides—a sleekness in the green hair of the well-groomed land—not ugly, not unpleasant to the sight when the sun gleams out upon it, and the cloud-shadows give the only variety possible to it—that of soft and tender gradations. But even in this beauty which remains to us—this mere surface beauty—there is a great snare, and danger, and temptation. Many of our artists are ruined by the pursuit of it, and others partially vulgarised. Sleekness and fat are always dangerous qualities for an artist to give his attention to, because sleekness leads to a kind of polish which introduces some confusion into the expression of the form, and fat conceals the bones and muscles on which the expression of energy depends.*

The finest cattle for artistic purposes in the United Kingdom are the little Highland breeds. Rosa Bonheur found this out very speedily when she visited Great Britain, and painted them with great enjoyment and success. Her 'Morning in the Highlands' and 'Scottish Raid' have one source of interest which does not exist in her famous 'Ploughing' picture: I mean, that of variety in colour. In many breeds of cattle one colour seems to be the rule, whilst any deviation from it is an exception. For example, in the celebrated and most valuable breed for working purposes—the *charolais*—almost all the animals are of a creamy white, passing occasionally into delicate shades of pale brown, but never offering any striking or picturesque contrasts. Our Highland cattle, on the contrary, are marked by the most striking variety; so that if you see half-a-dozen of them together in a Highland foreground, the chances are there will be at least three different colours—a red beast, a tawny beast, and a black beast; and there is nothing undecided about the colours either; but each is as frank in its own way as gules and sable in heraldry. To see a

---

* So in wood-carving, varnish or polish of any kind is barbarous; but when the carving itself is rude it may be varnished with advantage, because then the glitter partially hides the imperfection of the work.

group of Highland cattle just caught by the level rays of sunrise, when the cool breeze of the early morning is stirring the edges of their curly hair, all aflame with the first splendour of the day—when the black bull stands motionless beside his fair or red companions, who are glowing like images of pale or ruddy gold—is beyond comparison the most effective colour-combination ever to be had amongst the animals of Europe. So effective is it as to spoil one's eye for all other cattle, whilst the memory of it remains vivid. What are the dull beasts of the south to us who have seen kine standing together, of which one was as the foam of the sea, another like leaves in autumn, and a third like blackest night?

And not only for their colour are our Highland cattle dear to the heart of the artist, but for the uncommon grandeur of their bearing. Living half-wild, in scenery which is altogether wild, often exposed to the fierce blasts that whiten the dark lake, and toss the snow in wreaths over the edge of the precipice, they have acquired after a thousand years of vigorous resistance to the hardships of such a climate a certain grandeur of manner, far removed from the sleepy stupidity that chews its cud by Dutch canals and the sedgy watercourses of southern England. They must have some tradition amongst them, I think, of a time when beasts of prey roamed over the Highland hills more terrible than the fox or the wild-cat, for to this day they stand prepared for the aggressor, and their sentinels snuff the air.

The influence upon human character of association with

different species of animals is often very clearly traceable. The difference between the French peasant and the French townsman of corresponding social rank, which is one of the most striking contrasts in character to be found anywhere amongst the people of the same race, is due in a great measure to the constant association of the peasant with his oxen. Oxen, to begin with, walk a good deal more slowly than men are generally in the habit of doing; and as you never can get them to move any faster for more than a minute together, it follows that their driver must walk at their pace, not at his own. Two miles an hour is their speed, and when you have got into the fixed habit, after years of such companionship, of sauntering along at two miles an hour, you are not likely ever to be particularly brisk, even at the best of times. The French peasant thus becomes habitually a slow person, not indolent, but so remarkably slow, that he always seems to need the goad as much as his own oxen. His idea about life is that it is a tune to be played in *adagio*. He has no notion of economising time by getting rapidly through small and easy duties; in fact, he considers time only in very large spaces, such as the space between seed-time and harvest, or that between the feast of some saint in the autumn and the feast of some other saint in the spring. I doubt if he knows that there are such small subdivisions as minutes, or if he does, he thinks about them no more than a village blacksmith thinks about the millionth of an inch. In all this he is the exact opposite of the fussy, petulant little clerks and shopkeepers in the town, who are never really happy till they are in a hurry of some sort, either genuine or fictitious, and who order about the people under them as if the safety of the universe would be compromised unless they accomplished some utterly insignificant duty with the celerity of a conjurer. Nor is the teaching of the ox altogether unprofitable. A certain dull wisdom is what his example inculcates, and I would rather learn in his school than in that of the squirrel or the monkey. He believes hurry to be a mistake, and will not fret *his* nervous system with petty anxieties about doing things just at the minute. He knows that by the steady pushing of his mighty head the work will be done at sunset, and if not just at sunset, then an hour or two later, in the twilight; and what matter? I cannot say that his companionship is a very strong stimulus to intellectual achievement of any kind, but he can give what many of us need much more, and that is calm. Many a time, when vexed or over-excited by labour or by care, I have gone into the stable near me where the great oxen are, and spent an hour or two merely looking at them, or drawing them. Gradually, in their society, a great calm steals over the ruffled nerves and soothes them, and it seems useless to vex the brain with thinking or the hand with toiling after skill. In this way, although oxen are not yet admitted to the suffrage in France, it may be quite seriously argued that they have an influence over the votes, and a great deal of the success of moderate candidates is due to it. The political opinions of the ox, if we may judge by the peasant who speaks for him, are opposed to novelties and enthusiasms of all kinds, being steadily conservative and monarchical. Sometimes when he is harnessed with a young skittish colt in front of him, which occasionally happens in the rural districts of France, I think as I see them, what a perfect type that *attelage* presents of the political state of the country. 'Let us be deliberate and moderate,' says the ox, 'and if we persevere, all necessary work will get duly done in time.'

There is not a beast of the bovine species more to be respected than the poor man's cow. Some poor old man or woman invests a fortune in a cow, and leads the animal to pick up its subsistence in the ditches, and on those sweet irregular little patches of verdure which are to be found in the country lanes. Now if an animal is to be esteemed according to its value to its possessor, what prize bull, what winner of the Derby, is so precious to humanity as the meagre cow that the old woman guards on the lane-side hour after hour as she ceaselessly spins from her distaff? Meagre the cow is, indeed; so meagre that you can study anatomy very satisfactorily by observing her, all the bones being so prominent that the least observant of students cannot miss them. There is no mistaking the position of the ilium, at any rate.

In writing about the bovines it seems as if it would be an omission not to speak of the most magnificent example of their strength, the rage and fury of the bull, but in these papers I intend to confine myself pretty strictly to what I have seen, passing only with the most rapid allusion what I have read of or heard about, else there would be no end to the subject. Now, I never saw a bull really in a rage except once, and then most of the time, as the reader will see presently, I necessarily had my back to him, and could observe very little. It fell out in this wise. The present writer was descending a certain most lovely trout-stream, in his canoe, on a beautiful morning in June. In one place the stream passed through a great park-like pasture, and in the pasture were a herd of oxen with a very fine tawny-coloured bull. This bull took offence at the canoe and became furious. He began by galloping alongside and bellowing, but afterwards dashed into the stream. Had he been a better strategist, he would have done this below me and cut off my retreat, but the road was open before me and I paddled for dear life. The bull got on astonishingly fast, though, in spite of the rough, stony river-bed. The water may have been seven inches deep, the current, luckily, rapid, but great were my apprehensions of grounding, for had I once stuck fast my enemy would have been upon me. At length we came to a deep pool, with a quantity of snags I slipped through these, but they stopped the bull, who floundered about for awhile, and by the time he got to shore again I was safe in an impenetrable cover. The reader will easily understand that I had something else to think of than making artistic observations. And the truth is, that unless an artist goes to Spain, and studies enraged bulls in the arena, himself in safety, he has not much chance of painting them otherwise than from imagination. It would be easy to launch out into poetical accounts of smoking nostrils, and bloodshot fiery eyes, and furious hoofs that tore the ground; but if I wrote in that strain it would be on the testimony of others.

Cattle have been associated with human history from the very beginning, and with the earliest human art, but if one attempted to trace them through literature, and sculpture, and painting, there would be no end to it. Much of the interest, however, with which educated people look upon animals which have long served the human race is legendary and traditional. I never see a very beautiful white heifer without thinking of an antique sacrifice; and when a noble ox passes us—the noblest in the herd—it is difficult for any one whose thoughts revert habitually to the past not to imagine him with gilded horns, garlanded, and led towards the altar near some pillared temple under the blue Grecian sky. The only sight of this kind which I have seen or know of is the procession of the fat ox at Paris, which, I believe, is sacrificial in its origin, and has descended as a usage after its first purpose has been long forgotten. I remember the huge oxen elevated on their chariots, entering slowly, high above the surging populace, the great court of the Carrousel. Then they passed close to the Tuileries, and stopped before the balcony, and the Emperor came out upon the balcony with his beautiful wife and the young hope of his dynasty, and the people were merry and shouted, and the beautiful Empress smiled, and Cæsar looked satisfied, and the juvenile

Cæsar laughed outright, and all was joyous and gay! Times are changed since then. In this month of January, 1871, neither Emperor nor Empress ever comes to the balcony of the Tuileries, but the palace is full of wounded; and no fat oxen parade the streets, but the people have two ounces of horseflesh a-day, and are devouring cats and rats! *

* The above was written during the siege of Paris.

CHAPTER VII.

ASSES.

THE world-renowned City of Lyons has many glories, —the ever-renewed marriage of the Saône and the Rhône, their departure together for the far Mediterranean, the Imperial street that Paris envies, the great 'Ascension' of Perugino, the pilgrim-haunted heights whence our Lady of Fourvières protects her faithful town, and looks beyond it across the vast and verdant plain to the snowy heights of Savoy. All these glories has Lyons, and rich fair women array themselves in her splendid tissues; those tissues that the sad-eyed weavers weave with delicate skilfullest fingers, till they are softer than English mosses, and brighter than tropic flowers.

And for one thing more does Lyons claim our admiration and our gratitude. I speak not now of the arts which appeal to the eye only, but of an artistic product which, though lovely indeed to the sight, is grateful to another sense also, and valuable for the sustenance of life. In section like dark-red marble dashed with white, it may be cut to an infinitesimal thinness, leaving a surface smoother than the finest veneers. In the mass it is closely wrapped in silvery foil, to guard against the influences of the air. In the sweetest associations of the memory the *saucisson* has its place. Weary after the morning's march, the tourist takes it from his knapsack, and lays upon his bread those dainty discs which are its slices. The strength of his youth comes back to him, and the Alpine snows no longer seem inaccessible. At the stateliest Imperial banquet the *saucisson* is not disdained. At the pleasant picnic by the shady river it is found in the welcome baskets. The angler has it in his bag, the shooter in his capacious pocket, the canoist in his Lilliputian cabin of stores. O *saucisson de Lyon*, sad is the moment when we cast the skinny remnant of thee into the stream; but the little fishes congregate eagerly to the banquet, and ask each other what noble animal has yielded his flesh for their feasting.

What animal? That which Töpffer appreciated, and Sterne lamented, and Cervantes gave to the immortal Sancho; the animal whose image the art of painting perpetually reproduces. In the choicest galleries of princes you shall find him faithfully portrayed, and the wittiest and wisest of authors have learned philosophy in his presence. No exhibition of pictures would be complete without his likeness, and the very cleverest of painters have found him an admirable model. Even mathematicians have not forgotten him, for is there not a bridge in Euclid which bears his honoured name?

It may seem a perverse way of beginning the present

chapter to celebrate the excellence of the *saucisson de Lyon*, which, although confessedly made of donkey, and raw donkey, is nevertheless, being dead, incapable of exemplifying the beauties of the asinine character, and the superiorities of the asinine intellect. Yet in this exordium I do but follow the practice of a most accomplished master of the literary art, whose articles are models of everything that is irreproachable in form. Sainte-Beuve acknowledged that in his criticisms he always began by saying what could be said favourably, and then proceeded to direct attention, very delicately and gradually, to those limitations, and even deficiencies, which necessarily accompany great qualities. Of the ass, when living, I could not conscientiously say much that is wholly favourable, but when he appears in the state of *saucisson* he may be praised without the slightest restriction. *De mortuis nil nisi bonum*, especially when they are good to eat. Whilst on this point I may add that during the siege of Paris, when the flesh of all animals went to the stewing-pans, and even the menageries were discussed gastronomically, the palm of excellence was awarded to the ass. He appeared on the tables of epicures, he figured in the '*additions*' at the 'Gilded House,' at the 'Three Brothers.' Is it not sad that he never knew the posthumous honours that awaited him ? Ill-used and insulted during life, appreciated only after death, his fate resembled that of many other philosophers whom the world treated unkindly, and those odour was thought to be sweetest when their voices were silenced for ever.

It may seem presumptuous to utter a novel doctrine which must necessarily imply that all our forefathers have been mistaken, but it really *does* seem as if the whole human race had misunderstood the uses of the ass. His flesh was so compounded by the chemistry of nature as to be perfect food for man, but his brain was contrived with such bumps of obstinacy and resistance that he is the most vexatious of all our servants. He ought to be permitted to enjoy in peace that purely contemplative existence for which his character is adapted, and then, before his fibre hardens by age, to be transferred, as painlessly as possible, to the cook. Everything in his behaviour points to this—his resistance to commands, his resignation to suffering, his love of quiet, his persistent objection to industry of all kinds. If Balaam's ass spoke plainly, do not other asses speak plainly also, generation after generation, although their eloquence is wordless?

It is popularly said that the ass is the poor man's horse, and that Nature in her bounty has given him this useful and uncomplaining slave. Then the donkey is praised for his sobriety, for his patience, for his strength, fortitude, courage, perseverance, and the rest. But is not the poor man's horse supplied already by many hardy little races of ponies, which are as easily kept as asses, and much more easily managed? Surely the poor man has afflictions enough in the world without being condemned to suffer from the plaguiness of asinine perversity? Providence never compelled the human race to attempt the conquest of the donkey. Horses were provided for us in the utmost possible variety, from the miniature Shetland to the gigantic English hunter; but men had an idea that donkeys must be useful in some way, and they committed the fatal error of riding and driving, instead of cooking and eating them.

The use of donkeys is almost as much a matter of fashion as the use of oxen in labour. In one country you find thousands of asses, and can hardly drive for half an hour on a main road without meeting a procession of them harnessed to light little carts or carriages; in other neighbourhoods the donkey is nearly unknown. The old town of *Beaune,* in the Burgundy wine-district, is famous for the multitude of its donkeys, and the satirical spirit of neighbouring villages has called the land of Beaune *le pays des ânes;* with some reference, it is believed, to the human inhabitants also. On the other hand, there are regions where the absence of the quadruped would afford no opportunity for a sly sarcasm of this kind. Yet there are poor men everywhere.

It happened to me a few years ago that a certain member of my household had an unlucky fancy for a donkey, and as I was supposed to be a judge of horses it was unwarrantably inferred that I must be a judge of donkeys also. It is scarcely necessary to observe, that beyond anatomical resemblance there is so little in common between the two animals that a far more experienced horse-dealer than the author of these chapters might commit a fatal blunder in the acquisition of an ass. However, yielding to persuasion, I went to a certain fair where the asinine race was sure to be largely and worthily represented. In one corner of the great public square, under shady Oriental plane-trees, I found about a hundred animals to choose from. There were neat little grey ones, scarcely bigger than a large mastiff; there were ugly middle-sized ones of the colour of *amadou ;* and there were handsome big ones of a rich dark brown, that a cardinal might have ridden in a procession. The little ones had a sharp look, and bestirred themselves when they were touched; but it seemed impossible that their tiny meagre limbs should do any serious work. The middle-sized breed was too hideous, although one old woman used her utmost eloquence in behalf of an especially ill-favoured specimen of that breed, which was to be sold along with her foal. The point of her discourse was the advantage of hereditary succession. I have no doubt the old woman was a monarchist, for she used the well-known monarchical argument, that if the mature personage be not of much value, there is a successor growing up by his side on whom to fix our hopes. 'You see, sir,' she went on, 'if you buy a donkey all by itself, when that one donkey fails you, where will you be? Reflect a little on the numerous accidents and dangers to which the life of an animal is ever exposed! He may be taken suddenly ill; he may fall into a hole and break his leg; sooner or later he may become the victim of wasting disease, and there is always old age and decrepitude at the end! Against all these evils, this beautiful young foal in a great measure guarantees you. In purchasing both animals you provide not only for the present but for the future also. L'ânesse,'—the scene occurred in France,—' l'ânesse, c'est le présent ; mais l'ânon, monsieur, *c'est l'avenir !*'

This last touch, however beautiful as a climax, was better suited to a Gallic than to an English audience. The previous eloquence had enthralled me, but the final blow, which was to have riveted my chains, shattered them and delivered me. And yet I might have done better to let myself be persuaded, and give heed to the counsels of the aged, even though not wholly desinterested. At a distance of twenty yards stood the noblest-looking donkey in the fair; a perfect painter's model, tall as a Savoyard mule, with a superb texture, like the texture of some precious fur: and a deep beautiful colour, in which intense dark browns and purples played together—a colour unknown in horses, and which the horse, with all his superiorities, has never equalled. There was an artistic touch of scarlet ribbon about the head, and purest white about the muzzle, to finish one of the prettiest pictures I ever beheld. Even the long ears were an ornament, and so soft and agreeable to the hand that it was a pleasure to caress them.

According to what the vendor had to say the animal's character was as lovely as his exterior. He was the sweetest-tempered, the most docile creature man ever possessed ; a child might play with him in the stable, a girl could harness and drive him. Would I come and see? I might see him in the stable ; I might drive him myself about the streets. I saw him in his stall, a little child came and played about his legs; the gentle creature regarded his infant friend with an eye as mild and benignant as it was beautiful. A little maiden came and harnessed him to a cart. I took the reins and drove about the streets. He was swifter than the flight of summer, swifter than the delights of youth! No cruel blows were needed, no whip, stick, goad, or other instrument inflicting pain. His only fault, if fault it were, was a certain eagerness, a too abundant energy. I became his happy owner, at the price of two hundred francs without harness. The harness, which was nearly new, I paid for extra, and at its full value.

Still there were doubts, and if I had known donkeys as well then as I do now, enlightened by a painful experience, one fact alone would have unsettled me. The sun shone in all his glory on the day when first we met, the roads were clean and hard, the air was fresh and dry. A donkey's temper is closely connected with the barometer; he is comparatively amiable and vivacious when the air is dry, but he subsides into sullen sluggishness under the influences of humidity. As to the state of the roads, he is delicate as a prettily-booted lady. Mud is his abomination; he cannot endure to splash himself, and will not trot on muddy macadam till compelled by the cruelty of his driver. Therefore, to try a donkey with a view to purchase, it is wise to choose bad weather, for then you will see all his faults; but if, on the contrary, you desire to sell, exhibit him when the sun is bright and warm, the air clear, and the roads in the best possible order. It is much to be regretted that no rule of this kind has hitherto been discovered for men's guidance in the choice of a wife. How greatly would the hazards of matrimony be reduced if young ladies would be good enough to display quite frankly their good and bad tempers according to the state of the weather! A prudent lover would then provide himself with a pocket barometer, and so arrange his visits as to study in turn all those varieties of disposition which at present he finds out later, when the clergyman has done his work.

Just at first my purchase was greatly admired, and I felt proud of his size and beauty. He was as strong as a small horse, and certainly as gentle as any creature could be. But one day the baker, who had possessed a hundred donkeys in his time, and knew the animal too well to be deceived, beheld my paragon, and shook his head with mild, compassionate smiles. 'That donkey, sir,' he observed, in the quiet tone of a master-critic, 'that donkey is a handsome beast, and very large and strong, but his proper work is to draw a laden cart at a walking pace. He never was meant to trot: he may trot now and then a little, but never in a regular way. What you wanted was a little trotter, and the smaller they are the faster they go.'

We were not long in finding a suitable name for our asinine Adonis. The damp weather came and all his energy departed. He had the awkwardness of the elephant without his intelligence, the slowness of the ox without his perseverance. John Bunyan, in England, would have called him Mr. Go-to-sleep-on-his-legs; we christened him *Dortdebout*.

Dortdebout, or Dordebou in the abbreviated form, was a perfect model or type of a breed of donkeys which, as the baker said, are useful for drawing heavy loads, but not to be relied upon for trotting. He had no vice, except a perfectly unconquerable obstinacy. He was neither irritable nor revengeful, and it seemed cruel to use him harshly, for he showed no trace of rancour. A mild, meek creature, incapable of malice, he gazed at his persecutors with soft dark eyes, as if in simple wonder that men could be so relentless. After receiving a hundred blows he would make a feeble attempt at kicking, but this never went any further than a perpendicular lifting of the hind-quarters, and a sudden switching of the tail. When in harness, and not fully convinced of the necessity for making the journey that lay before him, he always went straight to the ditch, as his safest place of refuge: but he did not lie down, as many of his brethren do, and he never broke a shaft or a strap. On a muddy road, and in a state of mental aversion from labour, his average rate of progression was a mile and a quarter per hour, exactly; and in cold rainy weather it was his delight to keep his persecutors as long as possible exposed to the rigours of the season. Occasionally, however, as if to prove that his slowness arose from no constitutional infirmity, but was merely the effect of his own good pleasure, Dordebou would rival for miles together the swiftest trotters on the road. Not a horse in the whole neighbourhood could leave him behind, in fair trotting, when the spirit of emulation induced him to display his skill. He was an admirer of female loveliness, both in his own race and in horses, and whenever a carriage passed which was drawn by an animal of the gentle sex, Dordebou, however languid and tedious before, became suddenly inspired by an unshakable resolution to escort that carriage to the very end of its journey. It appeared on these occasions as if his feet, like those of Mercury, had been endowed with wings; and had it only been possible, by some ingenious optical arrangement, to project the visionary image of a female donkey on the road immediately before him, ever advancing as he advanced, Dordebou would have astonished the world. Thus an artist, with the vision of the Ideal ever before him, surprises by the energy and rapidity of his career the dull laggards to whom that ideal is invisible. But Dordebou, alas! resembled rather those inferior artists who have only occasional glimpses of the Beautiful, and who quickly subside into habitual inertia.

It is several years since I had the honour of possessing Dordebou, but the man who bought him from me keeps him yet, and loves him. Dordebou is admirably suited for his present station in life. He draws a heavily-laden cart, and does not profess to be a trotter. His master walks by his side and encourages him with many blows. I meet the two sometimes and caress the creature's soft long ears for the sake of 'auld lang syne.'

The next purchase I made was a tiny trotting phenomenon, about the height of a table. Harnessed to a very light carriage she was pretty enough to look at; and as for going, I never saw living creature go with such perfect good will. The impression she produced on the mind was exactly that of a toy locomotive, so we called her Loco.

Dear little Loco, model of good temper and cheerful performance of duty, my heart softens to all thy race when I meditate on thy perfections! The animal knew no guile; it was in innocence like the lamb, in swiftness like the gazelle. Before a week was over Loco was a household pet. But so tiny a thing as she was could not, with all her good will, draw more than a very light weight. Her carriage was a toy, and if more than one person got into it she had to make painful efforts. Indeed it seemed absurd and wrong for a grown-up man to drive such a wee thing at all, and I never did so without conscious shame. The ostler at my accustomed inn is a strong, tall fellow, and every time he harnessed Loco it seemed like harnessing a sheep. Then the carriage was so very light that on one occasion it positively upset, like a crank canoe, merely because I sat rather too much on one side. On the other hand, although the best-tempered thing that could be, Loco was quite unfit to be driven by children, on account of her irrepressible ardour. So soon as she heard your foot on the carriage-step she set off at once, with a trot so rapid that her tiny legs went like semi-quavers in a *presto*. We compared ier to a toy locomotive, and the comparison would be still more accurate if we added, that when the steam was once turned on it was impossible to turn it off again. If you met an intricate crowd of carts, occupying (as they always awkwardly do) the whole breath of the highway, Loco would not slacken her pace on that account, but dashed with you into the thick of them. Her theory of the division of labour was that her business was to go, and yours to find the passage; so that you were constantly in the position of a navigator in Arctic seas, impelled amongst icebergs by an impetuous wind, whose incessant anxiety is to find an opening in time. Then if you wanted to stop to speak with any one, it was impossible. Nobody could stop Loco till she got to the stable-door. The two stable-doors, that at the inn and the other at home, were her two *termini*, and she knew no intermediate stations.

After finding a new and good home for Loco my personal experience as a donkey-proprietor came to an end, and I have little desire to extend it. It is simply impossible to ride or drive the ass with comfort. It would be great presumption to decide about the character of an animal after studying two specimens only, but it has happened to me to make acquaintance with many others, and I have never yet seen the donkey which could be guided easily and safely through an intricate crowd of carriages or on a really dangerous road. The deficiency of the ass may be expressed in a single word; it is deficiency of delicacy. You can guide a good horse as delicately as a sailing-boat; when the skilful driver has an inch to spare he is perfectly at his ease, and he can twist in and out amongst the throng of vehicles when a momentary display of self-will in the animal would be the cause of an immediate accident. The ass appears to be incapable of any delicate discipline of this kind. He may be strong, swift, courageous, entirely free from any serious vice, but he is always in a greater or less degree unmanageable. When he is really vicious, that is another matter. There is no end to his inventions, for he is quite as intelligent as the horse, and a thousand times more indifferent to man's opinion or man's punishment. I have seen a donkey feign death so perfectly as to take in everybody but his master, who had been too often a spectator of that little comedy. Many asses are dangerous biters. It is probable that the idea of using the ass for service would scarcely have occurred to any modern nation if it had not come to us from the East. In hot sunshine the ass is at his best, and in the dry atmosphere of Palestine or Egypt he may display a permanent activity. Besides, in those countries he has the immense advantage of possessing a foil to set off such merits as are really his. People who are accustomed to the camel, the most stupid of domesticated brutes, may admire the ass by contrast, as Sir Samuel Baker did. And there are races of Oriental asses far superior in elegance to ours, and superior perhaps in delicacy and docility.

CHAPTER VIII.

PIGS.

ALTHOUGH in every country the upper classes fancy themselves to be incomparably more refined than their humbler brethren, more delicate in their tastes, and especially more fastidious in their invention or selection of verbal expression, it may be doubted whether, with reference to the valuable animal which is the subject of the present chapter, the aristocracy of any country upon earth is so elegant and even dainty in the use of language as the ignorant peasantry of France. The present chapter will doubtless have amongst its readers many ladies and gentlemen who never, from the beginning of a year to the end of it, do or say anything that violates such laws of good taste as are held to be authoritative in the English aristocracy; and yet I have heard English ladies of quite august rank and title, and of the most delicate breeding possible, say a word which no peasant-woman in Burgundy would utter unless the fury of uncontrollable anger made her temporarily forget all tradition of good manners. I have heard them say 'pig!'

It sounds innocent enough in English, but in France most people think it better to avoid the corresponding word, and so call the creature a 'pork.' The peasants go a step further, and avoid not only the word which begins with a *c*, but the other also. In their different *patois* they have names for the animal which they can use, it appears, without shocking their own fastidious ears, but when they speak pure French they use a periphrasis of quite remarkable elegance, hitting upon the only peculiarity about a pig which reminds one of genteel society. They call him *un habillé-de-soie*, a *dressed-in-silk*. And such is the force of the association of ideas, that every time I have lately seen advertised in the newspaper the title of a contemporary work of fiction 'In Silk Attire' it has conjured up in my imagination the vision of a large fat pig, all covered with beautiful white bristles shining in the sun like those wonderful silken tissues that ladies wear or long for.

This careful avoiding of the French word for pig that begins with a *c* (the reader may observe that I dare not even write it myself, though I hear the sound of it inwardly, which is almost as bad), is due to the fact that it has so often been applied to men of improper life. For instance, a powerful sovereign walked in the wood with his beautiful partner, and they met a child so lovely that she stopped to caress it. At length she added, 'This is His Majesty, wilt thou also kiss His Majesty?' But the child made answer that he would not, '*parceque Papa dit que c'est un*—' dressed-in-silk. And this is the way that the character of a truly respectable animal has been degraded in popular estimation.

The uncleanliness of 'the silk-attired' is not moral, it is merely physical, and a great deal is to be said in palliation of it. The brilliant historian, Michelet, restored his health and the vivacity of his genius by mud-baths, which in certain cases, are strongly recommended by the faculty. The reader of M. Michelet's later productions may not be aware that his clear and sparkling ideas are due to the practice of bathing in a medium so foul and opaque; and the pig, who from time immemorial, by his own unaided intelligence, without the advice of doctors, has cheerfully gone through the same treatment, may have derived from it inestimable benefits, physical and intellectual. Indeed, it may be argued that the pig's delight in mud-baths is really caused, not by love of dirt, but by a philosophical conception and aspiration after cleanliness, which makes him indifferent to appearances whilst he secures the reality. In the absence of soap the cleanly traveller finds a substitute in sand and clay, and so it is with the inhabitants of our styes. It is a fact that pigs are generally much less infested with vermin than many animals which are popularly supposed to be far superior to them in the decencies and elegancies of life. Mud is their soap, their worst fault being that, like little shiny-faced grammar-boys, they too often forget to wash the soap itself away when its purifying work is done. It must also be admitted that they are not always very particular in the choice of the soap itself. It is seldom perfumed; it is often not even pure. On the other hand, it is right to mention the well-known peculiarity of the pig, that he is much less indifferent than the horse or the ox to the condition of his bedding. These animals have no more objection to manure than an agriculturist, but the pig is delicate on this point in his own habitation, and likes to keep his bedding decent. It is evident also, that, however much we may differ in opinion from him on the subject of smells, his sense of scent is quite as exquisite as our own, for he can find the truffle by the help of it like the truffle hound, and is regularly trained for that service—a fact which ought to ensure him the grateful esteem of gourmands, since not only does he himself supply some of the best of animal food, but also by the perfection of his organs discovers for them the most delicious of all vegetable substances.

The habit of calling him 'the silk-attired' arose from a feeling of respect, not so much towards the animal himself as towards the ears of polite society. But as a skilful billiard-player sometimes aims at the cushioned side of the table in order to hit the balls the more effectually, many names have been applied to the pig without any intention of injuring *his* good reputation, but rather with a view of creating a converse association of ideas unfavourable to some human individual or class. It is a very common practice in France to call donkeys 'ministers,' not with any purpose of slighting the Protestant clergy, as such an appellation would certainly be interpreted in Scotland, but as a satire on the gentlemen who, for the time being, hold the portfolios of war, agriculture, public instruction, and the rest. And though it may be quite contrary to the rules of logic to infer that because some donkeys are called ministers, therefore all ministers are donkeys, the humorous and habitually-rebellious public enjoys a pleasantry which casts a disparaging reflection upon those in authority over it. In like manner a certain Count relieved himself to some extent of his feelings against the Government of National Defence by calling one of his pigs 'Gambetta,' and another 'Monsieur Favre,' always pronouncing the title *Monsieur* with well-feigned ceremony and respect. Some adopted a more generally inclusive system, and called all their pigs 'citizens'—a satire on red republicans which may not be very dangerous in these comparatively lukewarm times, but which in the first more energetic revolution would have cost the satirist his life. A man was guillotined near Autun, in the year 1793, for having made this jest in a less offensive form, since he did not elevate his pig to the dignity of citizenship, but a favourite dog, his beloved friend and companion. In times before modern revolutionary ideas were thought of, the pig was not unfrequently resorted to for the purpose of satirising the powers that were—even the sacred spiritual powers. Amongst the tales of the Queen of Navarre there is a story of two Franciscan monks, which is founded on this popular habit. 'There is a village,' wrote her Majesty, 'between Niort and Fors, called Grip, which belongs to the Lord of Fors. It happened one day that two Franciscans, coming from Niort, arrived very late at Grip, and lodged in the house of a butcher, and seeing that between their chamber and that of the host there were nothing but boards badly joined, they had a mind to listen to what the husband was saying, and so put their ears to the partition close to his bed's head. 'Wife,' said the butcher, 'I shall have to get up very early to-morrow morning to go and see our Franciscans, for one of them is very fat, and that's the one we must kill. We will salt him at once, and he will be profitable to us.' And although he meant his pigs, which he called Franciscans, the two poor monks, who had overheard this deliberation, were assured that it referred to themselves, and awaited the day's dawn in fear and trembling. One of the two was extremely fat, and the other thin; the fat one desired to confess himself to his companion, saying, that a butcher who had lost the love and fear of God would knock him on the head with as little hesitation as if he had been an ox, or other beast; and seeing that they were shut up in their room, from which there was no issue but that of the butcher, they might consider themselves sure of death, and recommend their souls to Heaven. But the young one, not so much overcome with fear as his companion, said, that since the door was shut, they must try to get out by the window, and seeing that it was not too high, leaped down lightly and fled as fast and far as he could without waiting for the other. Instead of leaping, the fat one fell heavily, and hurt his leg. Seeing himself abandoned, and unable to follow, he looked about him for a hiding-place, and saw nothing but a pig-stye, whither he dragged himself as well as he was able. Opening the door of the stye, he let out two great swine, and took their place, and shut the little door behind him, in hopes that when he heard some passers-by he might call to them for help. But so soon as morning came, the butcher sharpened his great knives and came to the stye, and cried aloud in opening the little door, 'Come out, my Franciscans; come out; it's to-day that I shall have your black-puddings!' The Franciscan, not being able to stand upright on account of his wounded leg, came out of the stye on all-fours, begging for mercy as loudly as he could. And if the poor Franciscan was in great fear, the butcher and his wife were not less so, for they believed that Saint Francis was angry at them for having called a beast a Franciscan, and fell down on their knees before the poor friar, asking pardon from Saint Francis. At last the friar, perceiving that the butcher would do him no harm, told him the reason why he had hidden himself in the stye, whereby their fears were converted into merriment.' Her Majesty goes on to narrate, in the most circumstantial manner, that the other friar fled all night long, and arrived at the Castle of Fors, where he lodged evidence against the butcher; whereupon the Seigneur of Fors sent to Grip to ascertain the truth, which being known, he told the story to his mistress, the Duchess of Angoulême, 'mother of King Francis, first of the name.' From all these details, the locality, too, being given (you will find the village of

Grip in any good map of France, in the department of the Two Sèvres), it may be presumed that the incident was not invented by the royal narrator, though artistically recounted by her, and possibly a little embellished. The retreat of the Franciscan into the pig-stye, and the scene of his discovery there, are probably 'unhistorical,' as modern criticism has it. But historical or not, it is a good story, and the indulgent reader will pardon the introduction of it here. *Je croy qu'il n'y a ny sages ny fols qui se sceussent garder de rire de ceste histoire.*

Yet how good soever the story may be the reader seeking instruction concerning pigs may reasonably complain of me that, like a certain Franciscan '*plus enlangagé que docte*,' who told tales in the pulpit instead of edifying his hearers, I am wasting time in vain discourse. Therefore let me hasten to prove how eminent must be the intellectual * and moral capacities of the pig. An animal which was the chosen friend and companion of one of the most respectable of saints, a saint especially famous for his steadfast resistance to temptation, Saint Anthony, can scarcely be unfit society for any Christian. It is on record, too, that when the demons tempted the good saint they plagued his pig at the same time, catching it by the tail, and playing it many other evil tricks, yet

* As to his intellectual qualities we know that there have been several instances of clever pigs exhibited in shows, pigs of genius, which had been taught to distinguish letters and cards. However, I never met with one of these animals, and have not an authentic account of one at hand. The phenomenon of genius (marvellously exceptional endowment) occurs probably in many races of animals.

the pig remained faithful to his saintly master notwithstanding the remarkable inconveniences of such association. The demons singed him whilst yet alive, and they made a horrible ring-dance with the pig in the middle, compelling Saint Anthony to exercise himself as one of the dancers:—

*'Faisons-le danser en rond
Tout autour de son cochon!'*

No doubt Saint Anthony loved his pig with an affection far more honourable to both parties than the love which men commonly bear towards 'the silk-attired.' As an illustration of the latter and less ennobling sentiment, I may mention a capital picture by Marks, in which that charming and original artist, with the quaint humour which is peculiarly his own, depicted a scene which he was pleased to entitle 'Thoughts of Christmas.' A monk wandering amidst great boles of ancient trees stops to gaze upon a herd of swine, rapidly fattening, and in the anticipatory expression of his countenance we read Christmas thoughts of a character rather gastronomical than religious. The way in which people look at and talked about swine, so exclusively from that monk's point of view, as if the sole end of their existence were to be eaten, is peculiarly repugnant to a student of animal character, and would be equally unpleasant to the pig himself could he understand the conversations which are so commonly held in his presence. Saint Anthony, no doubt, could have told us many things concerning his pig beyond the simple facts of his age and weight, which are all that farmers and housekeepers seem to care about. Saint Anthony would have enlightened us as to the pig's ideas, sentiments, affections, and we should have had a true portrait, drawn from long companionship and familiarity, not of the pig in general, which anybody may describe in a rough way, but of an individual porcine character which had no doubt its own delicate traits and interesting peculiarities. Do you suppose that the saint could ever think of his pig as so many pounds of ham, bacon, sausage, brawn, lard, black-pudding, and the rest? No, Saint Anthony was not a cannibal; he never thought of putting his friend into a flesh-pot, and, though having always at his side the living materials of a feast, he fed like a true hermit on innocent fruits and fair water:

> 'And they loved one another
> Like sister and brother.
> Wasn't it better to do so?'

The unfeeling heartlessness of housekeepers is well exemplified in the ferocious joy with which they anticipate a pig-killing. Mr. Marks could give his monk a speaking expression, but he could not make him actually talk as you may hear housekeepers talk. Some of them even go so far as to declare their intention of 'killing half a pig' next winter. Now what instance of cruelty to animals can be matched with this? It conjures up the most horrible images, like the phantoms of a ghastly dream. Which half of the pig is to be killed, and which to be left alive? How is the animal to be bisected so as to cause the least amount of torture to the half which must live and suffer? If this is horrible, the murder of a whole pig, as usually practised, is scarcely less so. The day of his death is a day of light merriment and jesting. He utters the most piteous cries, but no man regards him. He is taken for the last time from his little home, his stye, and cruelly bound till he cannot stir one of his limbs. And then the great knife is sharpened, the murderer feels its edge, smiling grimly, the idle servant-maids look on, gloating over the spectacle, the knife is plunged through many an inch of fat and flesh, the red blood spirts and gushes and is caught by sanguinary beings, with horrid eagerness, for their own devouring! After the sharp pain comes the deadly languor, after the cries of despair the silence of dissolution. Then the jesting of the bystanders seems louder, and they singe 'the silk-attired' with flaming straw, or scrape and shave him till his body is like a curate's chin on Sunday morning. And now that he is dead is he not truly a benefactor to humanity? Every atom of him is good for food. His body is so valuable that it pays all his debts, all the long account that has been gradually accumulating against him. Nay, there is even a considerable balance in his favour, and he bequeaths to his murderer a legacy of silver and gold. The idlest and most gluttonous of pigs need never fear that the stain of insolvency will attach to his memory after death, in which he has an immense superiority over anxious and improvident men. If his creditor ever reminded him how costly was the gratification of that fine appetite of his, he might answer ' *habeas corpus*,' and go on stuffing himself with a clear conscience.

Amongst many odd and ludicrous incidents which relieved the long tragedy of the Franco-German war, I may mention the quite novel and remarkable honours which in some instances were paid to the mortal remains of ' the silk-attired.' The German soldiers, whose powers of digestion would have excited unqualified admiration if they had not at the same time been the terror of all economical housekeepers, had an especial taste for pig in all the various forms which the art of the pork-butcher has invented. It became therefore a question which taxed the utmost ingenuity of the French, how to keep their pigs for home consumption after the departure of the devouring enemy. A lady whom I know conceived the idea of placing her pig under the protection of the Blessed Virgin, which she successfully contrived as follows :—First she killed it, and then, having salted the meat, put it in barrels which she interred in a corner of her garden. After that she invested a small sum in the purchase of a plaster Virgin, and erected a rustic altar above the spot where piggy slept in peace. Behind the altar the gardener arranged some pretty rock-work with moss on it, on a niche whereon the Holy Virgin was honourably installed. The invaders came; they probed the garden everywhere with iron rods—everywhere except in that sacred corner which the holy image effectually guarded. 'It is here that I pray,' said the lady, looking most pious, and the simple Germans respected the place of her devotions. A pig-owner in another department went a little farther even than that, for he laid out 'the silk-attired' on the best bed in the house, and covered it with white sheets with such art that the body presented quite the appearance of a defunct fat Frenchwoman. Round the bed he placed lighted candles, and by the side of it grave-faced watchers in the deepest mourning. The Prussian soldiers made themselves at home in the other rooms, but they respected the chamber of death, and as their stay was short, much bacon was economised by this stratagem.

A hideous custom used to prevail in many places, by which sucking-pigs were roasted whole and served at table without disguise. I knew a country gentleman who, being blessed with a fine litter of fourteen, sold them to fourteen different friends of his (he had many friends), with the condition in each case that he should be invited to dinner when the animal was to be eaten, a condition willingly accepted by the purchaser. It was not, however, from a love of sucking pig, but from a love of society that this ingenious conception originated.

Other charms than gastronomical ones have been discovered in young pigs by those who have occasionally made pets of them. The animal, though obstinate and self-willed, is really not stupid, and is capable of the warmest attachment, and of great fidelity to those he loves. All young animals are interesting, but young pigs are more comical in one respect than kids, or lambs, or kittens, or puppies; I mean, in the ludicrous combination of heavy structure with immense activity and precipitation. They are prudent in an advance, but they always lose their wits in a retreat, and on any decided alarm they hurry away in a general *sauve qui peut*. In maturer years an obstinate courage frequently developes itself, and they charge with such force that a man cannot resist them without using deadly weapons. I remember trying to get a pig over a bridge; we were three men against him, all armed with sticks, but he charged us so fiercely, that after an hour's hard work, and a hundred ineffectual attempts, we were compelled to give in at last, and his owner had to seek a wide bridge higher up the river which took him nine miles out of his way. On this occasion the animal displayed splendid courage and indomitable resolution, so that it would have been impossible to thwart his purpose without inflicting some serious injury.

The pig has not been so much painted as he deserves,* which is somewhat remarkable, for he is decidedly a

---

* It may be observed in passing that the pig is an important contributor to the fine arts by his bristles, which make the most suitable brushes for oil-painting. This may seem a small matter to the uninitiated, but the truth is, that the direction of a school's practice is in a great measure technically determined by the quality of the brush which it prefers. Hog-tools favour a manly style of painting, sable-tools a more effeminate one. I knew a Scottish artist of great merit who used to de-

popular animal, and some breeds of pigs offer very fine pictorial material, with rich blacks, and good flesh-colour and texture; besides which there is a great deal of character in their attitudes, especially in their perfect expression of repletion whilst the great business of digestion is going forward. Morland understood pigs, and his clever pictures of them found an appreciative public. But the tendency of modern breeding is, as usual, against the pictorial qualities of the animal. The prize-pig ideal is a round mass of matter like a gorged leech, with legs so small as to be scarcely visible, and so nearly useless as to be incapable of activity. The true pig, kept of yore in vast numbers by the swineherds of Gaul and Britain in the primeval forests, may not have been a pretty animal, but he had many of the fine qualities of his ancestor the wild boar, and something of the sublimity of his aspect. The best pigs for a painter to study are those which have deviated least from the natural type, those which have retained much of its strength, courage, and activity, with something of its fiery anger and ferocity. They plough the earth as if their snouts were of iron, they crash through the underwood like young elephants, where the acorns lie thick in the winter! Paint them so in the early forest, watched by the skin-clad swineherd, when the wild boars came out in the moonlight, and said, 'Let us play together!'

clare that oil paint could not be properly manipulated by any other than hog-tools, and that a school which used sables was inevitably on the road to a sure and swift decadence.

CHAPTER IX.

WILD BOARS.

I KNOW a little farm-house, in a lonely dell of the Morvan, where the unlucky tenant is plagued by two sorts of unpleasant neighbours, vipers and wild boars. The vipers keep him and his family in the continual expectation of being poisoned, and the wild boars are rival agriculturists, ploughing the land in their own fashion, and enviously damaging the crops. The farmer's lads keep watch and ward against these intruders throughout the nights of summer, whilst the corn is ripening in the tiny fields between the steep hill-sides. Dense is the forest to right and left for many a lonely league, and how many wild boars are hidden in those hills and vales of verdure not even the hunters know. Wild as they are they like the farmer's fields, and frequently in the twilight they may be seen venturing beyond the edge of the dark forest, and even when the moon is high their sombre forms move out upon the lighted spaces of the land. In a comparatively limited extent of country ninety of them were killed in a single season, in fair hunting, with horn and hound. Occasionally, but rarely, they leave their native forests on the hills and explore the fertile populous plain, miles from their lonely fastnesses. Only the other day, in the burning Burgundy summer, a wild sow and two young ones were imprudent enough to come near a certain château that I know, whose owner is an idle man surrounded by dogs and guns. Notwithstanding the torrid heat a chase was rapidly organised, and the cry of dogs, the galloping of horses, the music of echoing horns, resounded over the unaccustomed fields. Two days after I called at the same château, and the master thereof greeted me from the top of his outer stair with the grand old royal exultation, 'Hang thyself, brave Crillon; we have fought at Arqua, and thou wast not there!'

The old French nobility decorated the pursuit of the wild boar with a vast deal of external poetry. The elaborate and imaginative vocabulary of the hunt, the quite peculiar and original music, the picturesque costumes, the fanciful names given to the huntsmen, all derived from the chase itself or from sylvan nature, made the sport of the *grand seigneur* as much more splendid and romantic than the simple killing of a beast as is a princely banquet to the plain satisfaction of hunger, or the sculptured front of a palace to the wall of a Highland hut. Never was there a more perfect illustration of the philosophy of the superfluous! Of all those complex inventions and arrangements hardly one was absolutely necessary, yet each had a sort of reason for existing, deep in the recesses of the human imagination. It was like the ceremonial of a court, or of pontifical high mass, where many persons unite to produce an effect of collective discipline and grandeur, yet of whom the large majority are, like the actors in a theatrical army, costumed supernumeraries. It was barbarous, if you will; but if you take away everything that can be called barbarous, how little will be left to look upon! The exact opposite of it may be noticed in the matter-of-fact language and habits of English officers in India. The intense realism of contemporary Englishmen, their horror of anything like pageantry in action, or poetry in expression, produce a disposition the very reverse of that which adorns all human enterprise with the fanciful embroideries of romance. Instead of riding forth in three-cornered hats, in green hunting-suits faced with scarlet and gold; insted of encumbering themselves with enormous horns, those practical Englishmen go out dressed like jockeys, each with a plain spear; and even the Viceroy himself, lord of an empire tenfold greater than the France of Louis XIV., is not to be distinguished from the rest. And so far from using the picturesque old vocabulary of the chase, they will not even use the ordinary language of Englishmen; they reject it, not as too prosaic, but as not being prosaic enough. If an art-critic had to speak of a certain picture by Snyders, he would call it a boar-hunt, but our officers in India call it a pig-sticking. How perfectly that paints the strange shyness of the modern Englishman, depreciating his own exploits and his own foes, calling wild boars pigs, and the princes of India niggers, and himself a pork-butcher!

The irresistible tendencies of the age are stripping our life, fast enough, of the little external poetry that remains to it, and the feeling of wistful regret for the romantic language and picturesque usages of the past, which in Sir Walter Scott produced the characters we all know and the fictions we all enjoy, may still pardonably find a lodging in the hearts of some of us. For me, though the actual slaughter of any poor wild thing is in itself a sight not pleasurable, I enjoy the princely spectacle of the chase. Let the reader imagine—I am describing from memory, not from invention—a grand old forest château standing lonely in the heart of apparently illimitable woods. It belongs to a famous name of the old noblesse, but the master has a palace within easier reach of Paris, full of modern luxury, and so this old château is now a mere *rendezvous de chasse*. From its turrets the Alps are visible over a sea of forest-covered hills. The rooms inside are lofty and vast, and scantily furnished with a few pathetic-looking old things. On the walls of many a chamber

> 'Flaps the ghost-like tapestry,
> And on the arras wrought you see
> A stately huntsman, clad in green,
> And round him a fresh forest scene.
> On that clear forest knoll he stays
> With his pack round him, and delays;

T

> The wild boar rustles in his lair—
> The fierce hounds snuff the tainted air,
> But lord and hounds keep rooted there,'

Even so they hunted the boar in the days of Henry IV., and to-day again the grass-grown court of the château will resound with impatient hoofs, and the horns will break the solemn silence of the woods. Long before earliest dawn the men have been out with lanterns, and the mute hounds called *limiers*, to seek for the track of the boar. They have found the track and broken a branch and laid it down for an indication. The October mist lies in the distant valleys, and many a carriage is rolling over the roads that it covers towards the old forest château. About nine o'clock most of the invited guests arrive, the men in hunting costumes, various and picturesque, the ladies in morning dress. The men mount their horses, the ladies get into their carriages, and the whole cavalcade moves along one of the many roads in the forest. Within a distance of some miles from the château, in every direction, all these roads are sufficiently well kept for driving, and each has its own name in white letters on plates of blue enamel, just like the streets of Paris. Without this precaution it would be difficult to give precise directions. The *piqueurs* and *valets-de-chiens* wear a quaint-looking uniform of blue with gold lace, and are mounted on powerful grey horses. It is charming to see them pass under the great beech avenues near the house, it is a series of complete pictures, as sun and shadow fall upon them from mighty trunks and through the golden autumn leaves. The French painters of scenes of this kind delight especially in the *valets-de-chiens*, who whilst on horseback hold several couples of hounds in leash, and when they have to gallop need strength and skill to manage both horse and dogs. The expression of their faces, and their attitudes in the saddle, are enough to prove that the task is not always easy.

Some couples of the best dogs are sent forward to rouse the boar, whose whereabouts has been pretty accurately ascertained. As soon as any one catches a glimpse of him you hear the *fanfare* on the horns, and the chase begins in earnest. Then comes a great deal of galloping along the roads, the carriages managing to keep up pretty well by taking judicious cuts. Everybody gets very much excited, but the chances are that the people in the carriages will hardly be in at the death; and even the horsemen may have to dismount and make their way on foot into some dense jungle of young trees where the enemy stands at bay. The old-fashioned method of closing with him at the end was to attack him with spears; and even to this day some bold huntsmen go at him with the bare blade of a strong knife or dagger, but the more prudent finish him at a safer distance by the help of unfair gunpowder. A great old solitary will choose the ground for his last fight like some desperate outlaw on whose head a price is fixed. He will make for some rough place, impenetrable to every other creature except the snake and the weasel, some barren stony desolation choked with briars, where the vipers breed in peace. His decision made, he turns upon the dogs, and then woe to the hound that attacks him! The poor brave dogs come on, and are ripped open one after another. An old boar has been seen, in such a position, with five dogs killed and twelve lying badly wounded on the bloody stones around him. This is the time when the hunter has need of all his courage and coolness, and all his sylvan skill. The beast weighs between three and four hundred pounds, and such is the impression produced by his strength and fierceness that the great, grim, bristling mass looks twice the size that it is. Once on an occasion of this kind, as the dogs were killed one after another, and it seemed as though all the pack would be successively massacred, the master said reluctantly, 'Try him with old Rovigo,' an ancient hound of fame, used for attack no longer on account of the infirmities of age. The dog was fetched to the front, saw with dim eyes the monstrous boar surrounded by prostrate victims, regained for an instant, like old Sir Henry Lee in 'Woodstock,' the decision and energy of youth, fastened on the boar's neck, and hung there till the great beast received his death-stroke. But he also, Rovigo, had met his fate that hour: his body had been opened by the boar's tusk, and whilst he hung on with terrible grip his own entrails were dragging along the ground. His sorrowing master decreed a sylvan law, observed to this day religiously, that whenever men met together to hunt the boar upon those lands they should solemnly drink to the honoured memory of Rovigo.

Sometimes in this way there occur both tragic and ludicrous incidents. The wild boar is dangerous even to men; and brave men, such as the present chief of the House of Savoy, take spear and hunting-knife, and dare him to single combat in his own fastnesses. If there happen to be large thick trees close by, the danger is not so great, for an active man may then avoid his charges as he would those of an infuriated bull, but when there is nothing but brambles the hunter needs all his presence of mind. M. de Montcrocq, who was *lieutenant de louveterie* forty years ago in the department of *Saône et Loire*, was remarkable for his coolness at these moments. His great delight was to be charged by the wild boar, and stop him in mid-career with a rifle-ball. One of his friends tells a story which illustrates the almost incredible coolness and precision of the man. They were hunting together in a country covered with holly and furze, when the boar charged M. de Montcrocq, which was exactly what that brave gentleman desired. When he considered the animal near enough, he fired, and the beast rolled over. The huntsman ran to examine him, but could not find the ball. M. de Montcrocq, as he walked up at his leisure, called out 'You will most likely find it somewhere near the left eye, as I took aim there.' The ball had entered the eye itself. Men of this quality were born to hunt noble game, but some others would more prudently act upon the advice tendered by Venus to Adonis,—

> 'But if thou needs will hunt, be ruled by me,
> Uncouple at the timorous flying hare,
> Or at the fox, which lives by subtilty,
> Or at the roe, which no encounter dare:
>   Pursue these fearful creatures o'er the downs,
>   And on thy well breathed horse keep with thy hounds.'

Let the timid and irresolute remember that description of the wild boar which the eloquent Venus gave,—

> 'On his bow back he hath a battle set
> Of bristly pikes, that ever threat his foes;
> His eyes like glowworms shine when he doth fret;
> His snout digs sepulchres where'er he goes;
>   Being moved, he strikes whate'er is in his way,
>   And whom he strikes, his cruel tushes slay.

> 'His brawny sides, with hairy bristles armed,
> Are better proof than thy spear's point can enter;
> His short thick neck cannot be easily harmed;
> Being ireful, on the lion he will venture:
>   The thorny brambles and embracing bushes,
>   As fearful of him, part; through whom he rushes.'

It is said that too much study of literature and the fine arts has a tendency to lower the natural courage of man, and weaken the force of his resolution. Perhaps the person of whom I am going to narrate a brief but authentic history may have read these counsels of Shakespeare's Venus, and taken them to heart; perhaps, without being himself an Adonis, he may have seen pictures of that lovely youth, whose marble limbs lay stiffening in the forest-glade, where the bristly beast had torn them. He may have reflected, that, although not gifted with that perfect beauty, his limbs were not less useful than if they had been cast in a god-like mould, and although no divine mistress would ever lament his death, he might be wept for by a homely wife.

The story, a perfectly true one, is as follows:—A certain French nobleman, who loved the chase, and regularly hunted the boar, became dissatisfied with his *piqueur*, and discharged him. There were many applicants for the vacant place, and amongst the rest a stranger, who talked so persuasively and so knowingly, that he was accepted in preference to men who had distinguished themselves in the field. The first day that the new huntsman occupied his post, nothing could be more satisfactory than his manner, which was that of a master of sylvan craft. Evidently he was a man of experience and ability in *vénerie*. All went well till the boar was brought to bay. This took place in the thick forest, and the spectacle was more than usually animated, for the boar was a grand old brute, and sold his life dearly. After he was slain it suddenly struck the nobleman that he had not seen his new *piqueur*—where could he be? had any accident happened to him? All present asked each other these questions; when at length Monsieur le Comte happened to cast his eyes upwards and perceived his piqueur *in a tree*, looking in his gorgeous uniform like a very rare bird indeed. The Count immediately covered him with his gun, and shouted, 'Come down at once, or I fire!' The brave huntsman descended, and then his master added, 'Now cut for it, and look sharp, or you will have a bullet in your back!' and away went the hunter, boots, cocked hat, gold lace, French horn and all, followed by shouts of derision. He ran so fast that he was speedily out of sight, and he ran so far that they who had been witnesses of his shame beheld his face no more.

A great boar-hunt took place last year in a neighbourhood very well known to me, and the unfortunate chief actor therein (not the wild boar) was one of my most intimate friends. He had been invited along with many others to meet certain princes and other great personages who had come hundreds of miles to have a lordly chase, in fullest pomp and pride. The day dawned propitiously, the ground was admirably chosen, the *noblesse* were all well mounted, the track had been easily found. In the midst of the country where the hunt was to take place, my friend had a beautiful estate, and there he posted himself with his son, both of them well armed with rifles. A man is apt to feel peculiarly at home on his own land, and as my friend watched in his own wood, he listened, perhaps with too willing and credulous an ear, to the advice of his own keeper. 'If any boar were to come this way, sir,' said the man, 'you may fire without hesitation, for the dogs have disturbed more than one, and the one that comes here cannot possibly be that which they are hunting.' Scarcely had the man uttered these words than there was a rush in the dense underwood, and a fine boar burst in sight, bearing down upon the little group with a rapid and alarming directness. Father and son fired together, and the brute rolled over, dead. When they had examined the wounds, and were congratulating each other on this brilliant feat of arms, a great noise came nearer and nearer, a sounding of fanfares on many horns, a yelling of dogs, a clattering of hoofs upon the turf. Presently the whole hunt was there and surrounded my wretched friend, pouring maledictions on his head. He had been guilty of worse than murder, he had privily slain the beast which was just going to afford brave sport to prince and noble. In the rage of their disappointment they overwhelmed him with the bitterest abuse, swearing at him as only disappointed sportsmen *can* swear at the miserable being that comes between them and the satisfaction of their instincts. For the rest of that day, and for many subsequent days, he bore in silence the burden of a crushing unpopularity. They dragged away the carcase of his victim, they did not send him one slice, they did not invite him to dinner. Alone they left him, to meditate on the enormity of his crime!

Not only sportsmen, but artists, may regret the extinction of the wild boar in Great Britain. There is an immense difference, in picturesque interest, between a boar-hunt in the Morvan and a fox-hunt in Yorkshire or Leicestershire. The animal himself is larger, more terrible, and though ugly, is better material for painting; the scenery of the hunt is rougher and wilder, the costumes are more quaint and picturesque. Still finer must it be when the bold King Victor

Emmanuel meets the boar in the valleys of Piedmont, and the grim old lord of the forest succumbs to the royal spear, the snowy Alps looking down on him as on his fathers for a thousand years. It is barbarous, if you will, and satisfies instincts which are a remnant of savagery in our nature, but it is nobler to go up to a fierce old boar, whose jaws are dripping with blood, whose tusk is as dangerous as the horns of a furious bull, than to course the timid hare that has no means of harming you.* It is not beauty alone which gives power and interest to art, sublimity affects us even more. The wild boar is not beautiful, but he is sublime in his lonely courage. The younger boars keep together for safety against the wolves, and form into a close phalanx, the smallest in the middle, but the old ones live alone, each trusting to own cool prowess, and not even the wolf disturbs him. When the dogs chase him he goes on without any panic fear, turning round occasionally to chastise them, and choosing his ground ere long to fight the last hard battle.

* The Imperial Court of Germany pursues the boar from time to time, but the animal is bred in a paddock, and turned out to be hunted, before which his tusks are purposely broken off, so that he may do no manner of harm. If the motive of this is a human care for the dogs, which are often ruthlessly sacrificed in other countries, nothing can be more respectable, but it certainly takes away half the dignity of boar-hunting by removing the element of danger. It has been observed, indeed, during the war in France, that although the Germans showed the steadiest courage on all occasions when it was really called for, they took the most prudent precautions when danger might be reduced or averted beforehand. This is laudable in so serious a business as war, which is always perilous enough, but in field-sports some danger is necessary to make them interesting.

When he dies it is not without honour, and art may worthily celebrate his end.

This gregariousness in youth, and solitude in age, might be a text for a disquisition on human society and solitude if there were room for it. Association and isolation, each at the right time, are good for men as well as for wild boars. There is a time to unite ourselves in compact companies; there is a time also—though this is less generally admitted—to face in the solemnity of solitude the grave problems of life and death.

CHAPTER X.

WOLVES.

THE extinction of Wolves in England for so many centuries past, has given them, in the popular mind, a sort of unreality. The wolf is a great hero of fables, and eternally associated, in the dearest recollections of us all, with the story of 'Little Red Ridinghood.' The newspapers make use of him occasionally for political purposes; Prince Bismarck, for example, is not unfrequently compared to the celebrated wolf who complained that a lamb disturbed the rivulet he drank from,—the lamb in these cases being Denmark, or some other small power, with which the great Chancellor finds it convenient from time to time to have a quarrel. Mr. Gladstone, as we all know, is a wolf in sheep's clothing; and even in the Church, the controversial papers affirm that there are wolves in sheep's clothing also. So that, notwithstanding all the wise precautions of King Egbert, there are wolves in England yet; and especially one very big, and terrible, and grim, and pitiless old wolf (old he is, indeed, old as humanity, and likely to last till humanity itself perishes), which thousands and thousands of people have the greatest difficulty, do what they can, in keeping from the door. Keep the wolf from the door, indeed! What is a mere material wolf, going on four legs, to that metaphorical wolf—Destitution,—that envelopes people like an awful void and vacuum, in which no human lungs can breathe? This is one of those instances in which the metaphor lowers, instead of enhancing, the effect intended, at least, for those to whom the zoological wolf is not an unfamiliar visitor. For you may shoot *him*, or hit him with a stone, or give him a kick, but how are you to shoot Destitution, or stone or strike that hideous, incorporeal spectre?

The reader has no doubt often met with wolves in menageries and zoological gardens, but in England we are not under any apprehension about meeting with wolves in a state of nature. I cannot say that King Egbert rendered an unmixed service to the island by the extinction of these animals, for although he tranquillised the minds of the inhabitants, he at the same time deprived them of a small ingredient of danger which is not without its charm. When you drive through a French forest on a winter's night, the interest of your drive is very greatly enhanced by the possibility that a wolf may make his appearance in the middle of the road, or that two or three of them together may take to pursuing you, in which case you may rely upon it that your horses will show their speed to the best possible advantage. I remember driving one night in France, on the skirts of a forest, a very lively horse indeed, when suddenly he became livelier still,—so lively, in fact, that it was scarcely possible to hold him, and would not have been possible at all had not the road been deeply covered with snow, that was still silently and drearily falling. It was between midnight and one in the morning, and nothing was in sight but the black edge of impenetrable forest, with here and there a bit of sedgy morass, and, on the other hand, miles of treeless land, all white and untrodden, stretching away till it joined the dark grey sky. Whilst endeavouring to restrain the horse's impatience, I began to have a sort of feeling as if our shadows accompanied us on that swift course, and yet our lanterns were not lighted and there was no moon, nothing but the steady weird light from the infinite white fields. I had a lady with me, a Frenchwoman, not wanting in courage, and she quickly laid her hand on my arm, and said '*Les Loups!*' Yes, the two moving shades were a couple of large wolves cantering silently in the same direction, and in a line strictly parallel with our own course, not pursuing us, but keeping steadily in the fields to our left. So we kept on for about a league, the horse half mad with fright, and galloping as fast as the snow would let him, and still the two black creatures to the left of us, keeping up with us as it seemed so easily, with that steady silent canter of theirs over the thickening snow! Whether they would attack us or not depended simply upon the intensity of hunger they might be enduring, and we watched them for some minutes with anxiety, but at length we began to imagine that the lines of our courses were no longer quite parallel, that the space between us and the wolves was gradually widening. Soon afterwards this became a certainty: the wolves were going on a mission of their own, probably to some sheepfold in the neighbourhood, and did not intend to honour us with their attention. The parallelism of our lines of route had been merely an accident, and our companions grew less and less, till at length we could only perceive two tiny black specks that seemed almost motionless in the distance, and that nobody who had not seen them nearer would have suspected to be wolves at all.

Sometimes, however, the wolves are more to be feared, even in France. It seldom happens that a man is in much danger from their direct attacks, but there is a great peril of a bad carriage-accident when your carriage is pursued by wolves. Horses have a perfect horror of these animals, and lose their heads entirely on such occasions; so that one has good reason to dread wolves when driving, especially if the road is an awkward one. I know a road through a forest in the Morvan that I should not quite like to drive over at midnight, after a long frost, when the wolves are hungry. The forest in that place is about nine miles in diameter, and the road, after passing through the densest shades, winds along the edge of a precipice on a sort of ledge or shelf, which has been blasted for it out of the solid granite.

There is a low parapet on the other side, and when the rock juts out towards the abyss the road makes a sudden bend outwards also, so that it is rather a dangerous place to drive upon even in the best of times. Well, it happened one winter's night that a certain man was driving over this lonely road through the forest in a sort of gig, quite by himself, when his horse suddenly became uncontrollable. The driver found out the cause very shortly, for a band of several wolves were in full pursuit. He had nothing to do but try to keep from upsetting, and let his horse go as fast as mortal terror could impel him. At length they came to the precipice, and here there is a rapid decline, as the road winds in and out upon the face of the cliff. The decline continues for miles, and the horse went down it at full gallop. Every time he came to a turn there were two imminent dangers, that of a collision with the jutting rock on the inside of the curve, and that of flying over the low parapet on the outside of it into the deep abyss below, where a mountain stream falls amongst its rocks in a series of wild cascades. The wolves got nearer and nearer, the wheels went faster and faster, bounding from the stones in the road as a boy's hoop leaps and springs. At length they were out of the forest, and the wolves began to drop gradually behind, a lonely hamlet was reached, and the pursuit ceased altogether.

Very often a wolf sets out by himself on a little excursion amongst the farms and villages, usually at night, occasionally, but rarely, in the day. When he prowls about a farm the animals fly in every direction; if any horses are out at grass they leap the hedges with an agility that you would never suspect; stiff old cart-horses even will try a jump, and blunder through the hedges somehow. As for the sheep, unless secure in a fold, they have an anxious time of it, and disperse themselves without calculating consequences, so that the next day it is not easy to get the flock together again, and if there are any streams it is likely enough that you will find a sheep or two drowned in them. When the wolves get into the habit of visiting a particular neighbourhood, they continue it for several nights almost consecutively, and the farmers there become very vigilant, getting all animals safely housed at dusk. The wolf comes into the farmyard, and the creatures in the buildings round it know that he is there, and pass wakeful and anxious hours. One night in winter, when there were wolves about the farm I live upon when I am in France, I went about midnight to the stable, and just on coming out of it met a fine wolf face to face. We were not more than six or eight feet from each other, and both rather taken by surprise. I had no weapon, but remembered the tradition that you must never turn your back upon a wolf, so I stood still and asked him what he wanted there. The sound of a human voice seems to have affected the wolf's mind, for he turned round and slinked away into the dark shades of a neighbouring wood. The morning after I learned that he had killed a goat on the next farm. I exactly remember what passed in my mind during our brief meeting. 'That's a large dog; no, it is not a dog, it is something else; what else?—wolf—no weapon—must keep my face to him.' Then

V

aloud, 'Well, sir, what do you want here?' On which he looked steadfastly at me for a second or two without stirring, then made a rapid right-about-face and cantered woodwards in perfect silence.

This meeting was rather a surprise, but a surprise of a still more startling kind happened to an old woman who was walking through a lonely wood. She felt two paws on her shoulders, and on turning round (which we may be sure the old woman did sharply enough) found that it was a very big wolf who had a talent for practical joking. After this the wolf followed her, quite closely, till she got out of the wood, and then left her, without doing her the least harm in any way. Now, although the pleasantry of laying two heavy paws in a startling manner upon an old lady's unexpecting shoulders cannot be considered in good taste, still we must make allowances for a facetious animal that could not express his facetiousness by language; and the perfect politeness with which he afterwards escorted the victim of his joke, though no doubt she would willingly have dispensed with his attendance, proved, I think, on the wolf's part, a degree of natural courtesy remarkable in a creature who could never have been much in the society of ladies.

In all these anecdotes which I have just been telling, the reader may have observed one common characteristic that nobody comes to any harm, and so it is in the vast majority of such instances. Wolves are not dangerous to man, except in bands and maddened by intolerable hunger. When the wolf appears in the day-time amongst the flocks of the Morvan villages, a vigorous young shepherdess will even go and kick him with her wooden shoes, and the lads, instead of running away, pelt him heartily with stones. The wolf in England, where he is seen in menageries, like a savage panther behind strong bars of iron, enjoys a much more imposing reputation than in France, where he is more familiarly known. Indeed the word *wolf* and the word *loup* do not convey the same impression to my mind, because ' wolf,' to me, is associated with the grand mystic conception of the animal, whereas *loup* is associated with the simple reality.

When a peasant can catch a wolf alive it is a source of profit, as it is the custom, in all the farm-houses he chooses to visit, to make him a small present. A man addicted to poaching, a clever trapper, managed to catch two wolves, and brought them to my house. They were of course very securely muzzled and chained, and cowed by what newspaper reporters would call 'a sense of their position;' but after making all deductions on that account I could not help thinking that for animals so celebrated in fable they cut but a poor figure. I was curious to see how my dog would behave in their presence, and called him. His conduct was admirable, he showed no more emotion than Sir John Malcolm did when he passed the Persian giant, whom he took for a painted representation of Roostem and his club, but passed close to the wolves with a mere glance at them and then lay down at my feet whence he contemplated them at his leisure. On comparing the dog and the larger of the two wolves, I perceived that Tom was certainly the heavier and apparently the more powerful animal of the two; and it is my belief that in a combat, unless the wolf gained at first a decisive advantage from that instantaneous ferocity of attack which wild creatures usually have in a superior degree, Tom would have had the advantage. According to Toussenel, however, who was an experienced hunter, dogs have a great objection to fight the wolf, and the best wolf-hound in the world will give in promptly when he is wounded. A famous wolf of the department of Saône-et-Loire which had lived in a forest near Cluny, and was known in the neighbourhood by a name, for the hunters called him *Cambronne*, would issue from his retreat when hunted and break a leg of each of the hounds with an astonishing rapidity. So at last it was decided to conclude a treaty of peace with Cambronne, and the hunters disturbed him no more. He met his death in a most strange manner. One day he was swimming in the river Saône when one of those long steamers that ply upon it overtook him and killed him with a stroke of the paddle. When the body was taken out of the water it was recognised as that of Cambronne. As to the strength of wolves, Toussenel says that he himself saw two wolves drag the body of a large mare, which weighed at least seven hundred pounds, out of a muddy marsh with sloping sides. They got it up somehow upon the dry ground above, and in three hours had eaten half of it. When you consider the size of the wolf, both these facts would be incredible if we had not the authority of a careful personal observer who took the greatest interest in the habits of animals. Supposing that the wolves weighed a hundred pounds each, their united weight would be two hundred pounds, and they ate nearly twice that weight of horseflesh in three hours. It appears, however, that they can reject their food at will, and in that way enjoy a gluttonous interminable banquet like Heliogabalus. The other fact that they drew the mare out of the marsh can be explained by nothing but vast muscular force and great skill in applying it.

The character and habits of the wolf have been carefully studied by many observers, who agree in admitting his craft and intelligence, though some of them doubt his courage. Toussenel tells us that he himself saw six full-grown wolves crossing the frozen Loire, in single file, in the winter of 1829, that he examined their track afterwards, and would have supposed, if he had not seen six wolves, that only one animal had crossed the river in that place, so accurately had the five others placed their paws in the foot-prints of the first. The wolf is so suspicious that it is almost impossible to poison him. If you place a poisoned carcase near his own residence he will not touch it, the only way to get him to eat of it is to drag it a long distance so as to make a trail, and then seem as if you had been anxious to hide it. He will follow the trail at night and find the carcase. A common way is to lie in wait for him with rifles round about the spot where the carcase is, and then pour a converging fire upon him the moment of his arrival. Notwithstanding the most intense hunger he will not eat of anything that seems to him suspicious, he will devour earth itself first. The same prudence marks his conduct in all respects; he will not uselessly expose himself, yet he is not a coward. Like all robbers he enjoys foggy weather, considering it to be favourable to his operations, in which he resembles a well-known London thief, whose most audacious feat was the successful robbery of a twelfth-cake from a confectioner's shop, under cover of a London fog. It is well known that a farm which is close to the wolf's private residence is safer than one situated at a distance of a few miles, as he thinks it best to avoid scandal in his own neighbourhood, just as young gentlemen conduct themselves very properly when at home in the country who are not always quite so good in London or Paris. The wolf knows too, very well, who are his active enemies, and who are the people whom, though not friendly, he can afford to regard with indifference. An instance is on record of a wolf which, quietly seated on a little eminence, watched the long line of peasants' carts going to market along the highroad close to where he was. The long procession amused him, just as it amuses an old lady sitting by her window, and no doubt he made his own philosophic reflections on a kind of life from which circumstances had excluded him. Hundreds of anecdotes might be collected in proof of the wolf's exceeding intelligence in all that concerns the preservation of his life, and every hunt supplies fresh examples. A family of young wolves, instructed by their mother, will mislead the hunters artfully, taking the dangerous duty by turns for the protection of the rest. But when a strong, full-grown animal gets fairly away, out of the ring of beaters, his policy is simple in the extreme. He chooses a straight line, and sticks to it across all obstacles with uncompromising rectitude, and the worse the ground the safer he is, for then the distance rapidly widens between him and his pursuers. When the hunters are far behind the wolf relaxes his pace to a quiet trot, and finally takes a rest, not troubling himself much if one or two of the foremost dogs reach him, for he will give them a sharp bite or two that will deprive them of any wish to vex him again. It is generally agreed in France that it is not of much use to follow a wolf with dogs alone, on the principle of English fox-hunting, so the hunters are armed with rifles, and if the wolf is killed at all, which does not happen in every hunt, a bullet is the invariable cause of death. But then in France they have not the true wolf-hound. In Russia and Poland they have better dogs very likely, but on this point I am not able to inform the reader, not having been in Russia.

It happens from time to time that an attempt is made to bring up a wolf like a dog. These attempts succeed up to a certain point. One of the most remarkable instances occurred in the neighbourhood of Bordeaux, where a *grand veneur* brought up a black wolf-cub, a bitch, along with his young dogs, in perfect liberty. She went out hunting with the dogs, and enjoyed the chase extremely, except when the purpose of the expedition was a wolf-hunt, to which she had honourable objections. She behaved charmingly in the kennel, and her only fault was sheep-killing, a crime she committed whenever the opportunity offered. A tamer of wild animals (Martin) harnessed a pair of French wolves to a carriage, and they behaved well when the voice only was used to command them, but when they heard the whip they snapped at each other with their teeth, and it appears that the sledge-dogs in the Arctic regions have the same characteristic. Indeed, it appears doubtful whether those animals, although we call them dogs, are not in reality a species of wolf. They do not bark, and according to Captain Parry their anatomy is exactly that of the wolf. This suddenness in snapping at each other under the belief that the whip stroke is a hostile attack on the part of their companion is strictly a wolfish characteristic. I have observed hybrids which were descended from an union of dog and wolf which it was most dangerous to caress on account of the suddenness with which they would use their teeth on the least suspicion of your intentions.

Though the wolf is a robber, and we do our best to prevent him from injuring the domesticated animals which belong to us and contribute to our wealth, it would be difficult for any just person not to have a feeling of great sympathy for him. The wolf in modern Europe, the last of the wild beasts dangerous to the larger animals and to man, is in a position as false as that of a baron of the Middle Ages would be if he could come back again to his castle in the middle of modern Germany. After all, the wolf has but one real fault, that of being a carnivorous animal, appreciating mutton, and unfortunately neither having money nor knowing the use of it, he is unable to go to the butcher as we do. Compare with him, for instance, the most refined and delicate of God's creatures,—a pretty young lady with a good healthy appetite, and no convictions on the subject of vegetarianism. She eats mutton, too, and many other kinds of animal food, only she eats them prettily with a knife and fork, and the mutton, &c., have been bought at a shop, already slaughtered for her use. The wolf has an appetite even yet more vigorous, and scarcely any legal means of satisfying it. He has no money, he has no profession, like the dog, by which to earn a respectable existence. When the long, terrible winter comes, he can only live by robbery, and can we blame him if he satisfies an imperious appetite, an appetite of an intensity probably unknown to any of us? He has to be his own butcher, and to snatch his prey from the hands of his deadliest enemies. In managing this he gives proof of infinite address, and a kind of prudent boldness which is the wisest policy for a creature in his situation. If he behaves distrustfully to man, has he not ample reason? What have men ever done for him or his race? Have they not hunted and persecuted him since the world began, stamped him out of existence in England, and in the rest of Europe driven him into the hungry wilderness? Fortunately for him he has the instincts of association, and so does not live utterly in solitude.

We have all of us read of those terrible occurrences in Russia when a pack of wolves pursue a sledge as harriers follow a hare. It is in scenes of that kind that the animal becomes truly terrible. There was a real battle between men and wolves in Russia in the year 1812, and the wolves gained an unquestionable victory, for they killed every one of their enemies, neither giving nor receiving quarter. On the field of battle after the combat there lay eighty human corpses, soldiers, their muskets strewn upon the snow, their bayonets red with blood, and round them a ring of two hundred wolves that they had slaughtered. I think that battle must have been the grandest to witness that human soldiers ever fought. Fancy it raging in the depth of that Muscovite solitude, man and beast—man and beast—man and beast in mortal combat, till the men had all fallen except ten, till of these ten there remained only five, three, two, one, and that last one fighting alone for the last minutes of his doomed existence,—alone with his seventy-nine comrades serving for a horrible repast around him, and the irresistible wolf-army howling, and leaping, and gnashing innumerable teeth!

In France there is little danger of such tragic events as this. There are really not very many wolves in France, certainly not enough to make dangerously large bands. M. d'Esterno calculates (on very certain data, since a reward is given for every wolf that is killed, and accounts are kept of these rewards) that 1860 wolves are killed every year in the whole country. Of these, 820 are cubs, and even the young adolescents (in French, *louvards*) are counted as old wolves, so that the real old wolves are not probably more than 300. After a calculation of probabilities with which I need not trouble the reader, M. d'Esterno arrives at the conclusion that the total number of births in the wolf-tribe in France in the course of one year, can scarcely exceed 3000. Now, since the area of France exceeds 200,000 square miles, one wolf is born every year in sixty-seven square miles of territory, which is not an alarming lupine population. Indeed, the wolf would be extinct in France already, were it not for an institution which was especially created for his destruction, but which has ended in his preservation. Certain gentlemen of fortune are appointed *louvetiers* (wolf-hunters), and the royal authority, which first instituted them, was supposed by loyal fiction to intervene for the protection of the peasant against a noxious animal. However, the fact is, that the *louvetiers* look upon a wolf precisely as an English gentleman in Leicestershire looks upon a fox. The administration of woods and forests, too, is favourable to the preservation of the wolf, because a forest lets better for shooting when wolves are known to exist in it; and a powerful administration of that kind has many means of influence. If a *louvetier* were to take his occupation seriously, and really try to exterminate the wolves, he would find himself hampered at every turn by a set of rules contrived for that special purpose. It is settled, for example, that a *louvetier* can only hunt in his own district, and that when he hunts in woods belonging to anybody else he can only do it on a day fixed beforehand, for which he requires a special permission from the prefect of his department. The chase, too, must be conducted in the presence of foresters and gendarmes. All these contrivances ensure the safety of the old wolves, which easily get out of the limits fixed, and have due notice, as they are not hunted when first discovered, and there can be little doubt that the whole official organisation is strictly wolf-conservative. If we had wolves in England, and were accustomed to the exciting sport which they afford, it is likely that we also should have an influential party in favour of their preservation.

I regret to have had so little to say in this paper concerning the wolf in fine art, but the fact is that with the exception of the she-wolf who suckled Romulus and Remus, of which an antique statue remains to us, and the wolves in great hunting-pieces in painting and tapestry suitable for the decoration of country-houses, the animal has not figured very largely either in painting or sculpture, and is not generally very intimately known to artists. English painters see him at the Zoological Gardens, Continental ones occasionally have the advantage of seeing him in his native forests, but only by glimpses. He is more useful in poetry than in painting, because when skilfully introduced in verse, he may be made to give very powerful effects of savage wildness. The association of his dreaded name with hungry solitudes, covered with inhospitable snow, with the desperation of flying steeds, with uncounted quantity of pitiless pursuers, makes it enough simply to mention him at the right time to enhance a poetical effect very cleverly; whilst such is the tradition of his fame that when your horse breaks into a wild gallop at wintry midnight, and your companion points to the next field and whispers, 'The wolves!' and you see them dimly in the pale snow-light, there comes a thrill, not so much of fear as of an old poetry that has descended to you through all the generations of our race.

CHAPTER XI.

KIDS.

EVER since men began to observe the ways of animals, and this is going very far back into the past, for mankind has loved and studied animals from its earliest infancy, they have recognised some marked moral characteristics as belonging in quite a special sense to each of the species which they knew. In the old fables which have come down to us through various transformations, the animals are, as it were, so many well-known characters in a little drama, each character being strongly marked by one or two striking traits which are never forgotten, and which universal consent has accepted as typically accurate. In the mediæval fable this dramatic arrangement of the animals most familiar to the people of Western Europe takes its most clear and perfect form. The animals become, severally, personages with names, and a style suitable to their supposed rank in the animal hierarchy. Neither the narrators of mediæval fable, nor their hearers, ever seem to have imagined the possible objection that there might be a variety of character amongst animals of one species. They simply took the species as a whole, fixed upon one salient characteristic, and gave this salient characteristic as the whole nature of the typical bear, or fox, or cat, who became Monsieur Berenger, or Maître Renard, or Madame Tibert. Then with the characters obtained by this process, they made up their little play, which had the immense advantage of simple *dramatis personæ*, easily remembered, each strikingly unlike every other, and, therefore, easily grasped by the popular intelligence and retained by the popular memory.

Now, this way of estimating the characters of animals is not a bad way to begin with, but it is altogether rudimentary. It is true, to a certain extent, that every animal is marked by some one of those characteristics which are to be found in the manifold nature of man; but no one who had studied animals could be entirely satisfied with such a rough indication of one salient attribute as a description of animal character. For example, in popular fable and tradition, the unlucky goat always stands for uncleanness, on account of an unfortunate musk-like odour, extremely powerful, and to us certainly most disagreeable, but which may be tolerable enough to organs differently constituted. This is man's way of settling the position of his fellow-creatures; he dislikes the smell of the goat, and accuses the animal of exceptional impurity, which accusation is otherwise utterly unfounded. It is to be regretted that we cannot learn the goat's opinion concerning the odour of man, for there is no doubt that man has a very strong odour, and one which is most offensive to many animals. It has been remarked farther, by naturalists, that this odour is not diminished by cleanliness, but is inherent in man's very constitution. I think, then, that this question of odour, as affecting the character of the goat, had better be left out of our calculations altogether, for there is nothing positive about an odour; it is merely a matter of relation between our olfactory nerves and the fine floating particles which excite them. The scent of carrion is unpleasant to me, but it is certainly not unpleasant to my dog; and he is quite as good a judge as I am, nay, probably even by far the better judge of the two, for his sense of scent is incomparably more exquisite, more true, more critical, more refined, and more reliable than mine. He can follow me through fields and woods, across a thousand contradictory scents, by the sole guidance of his nose; and I could not follow him a single yard by the help of my nose. Let us, therefore, learn a certain modesty in judging of other beings, which, though so near to us, and so much beneath us as it seems, and so entirely in our power, live in truth in so many different worlds. The goat lives in goat-world, the dog lives in dog-world, the donkey in donkey-world. What I should like to do for myself and the reader, if it were possible, would be to get a true glimpse or two of each of these strange worlds, so different from ours, and so difficult for the wisest of us to understand.

Thackeray used to contemn the indifference of certain wealthy families (who in this differed most widely from the lady who is the head of English society) for everything that concerned their servants. Not to know, or care anything about the poor people who live under our roofs, and do our work for us, and spare us every day a thousand annoyances, hindrances, and delays; making life quite smooth and easy for us, so that we have leisure both for study and for amusement; not to know or care anything about these people, to whose faithful service we owe so much (and we are often ignorant even of their very names), seemed to Thackeray a sort of plague-spot in our society, and a grievous scandal and wrong. In the same way I have often thought, whilst noticing the stupid and cruel way in which animals are treated; the almost constant habit of using them merely as things, and not as if they had the feelings and characters of individual beings, that we have other servants besides human ones, who deserve more consideration than they get.

Of goats in their maturity we shall have something to say in another chapter, but for the present I content myself with speaking of them in their infancy or kidhood. The main characteristic of the kid, considered individually, is his very remarkable precocity, and the surprising readiness with which he adapts himself to his new situation, and acquires the knowledge necessary to it. Early on some April morning, let us suppose, he finds his way into the world, just as the sun is beginning to drink the dew from the early flowers. For the first quarter of an hour he is uncomfortable enough, and looks, as he lies on the ground, from right to left in an unsteady and uncertain manner, his general appearance reminding one of a half-drowned rat still giddy from the effects of asphyxia. After a while, however, he gets up and tries to walk about a little; at first not elegantly, but somewhat after the manner of a school-boy upon stilts. For the moment the poor kid is a type of weakness aud inexperience; he staggers about like a kid inebriated, and hits his muzzle against any obstacle that may come in his way. He rapidly, however, in kid-fashion, acquires the precious science of perspective, and sufficiently explains to himself what those marvellous patches of colour all about him stand for. Very soon, of course, by the infallible instinct of nature, he finds his way to the maternal teat, and gets his first long, refreshing, strengthening draught of milk. The good that first drink does to a young kid is magical. After it he makes his first caper—the first of ten thousand capers—and becomes a new being. He begins to explore things, to wander about his mother's legs, which at first appear to him only in the light of pillars supporting a great milk-cistern, and to make acquaintance with his brothers or sisters, if he has any.

And now begins that beautiful fraternal life of the young kid, than which nothing in nature is more lovely. Suppose a litter of three kids all together. Of all types of tender brotherhood and sisterhood I think they are the most perfect. I knew a Scotchman who always called his children his kids, which, I believe, is not an uncommon practice in the south of Scotland and in Ireland; and since I have become more familiar with the ways of animals, the idea of kid life seems to me not at all a bad one to set before young children. With all the eloquence of gesture, and of the most beautiful grouping possible, three kids of the same litter continually express the fulness of fraternal affection. Why they love each other so very dearly, and as soon as they first really see each other, is one of the divine mysteries of the instincts, but it is so; there is no doubt or question about it. Their life is a sweet alternation of play and rest, play and rest, play together and rest together; nor can play more joyous, or rest more perfect, be found in all the realm of nature.

In their grouping, merely from the instinct of imitation, and, of course, without the slightest intention or conscious preference, they constantly arrange themselves with a wonderful and beautiful symmetry. If there are two kids, one puts himself in a certain position, looking, let us say, from the left of the spectator to his right; in this case the other is pretty sure to come and put himself exactly in the same attitude, but looking from right to left. If there are three kids, the third will make a centrepiece of himself, whilst the two others group instinctively as symmetrical supports. I have seen a hundred natural groupings of this kind invented by three kids which belonged to me last year, all of which were quite symmetrical enough in arrangement for the severest Greek ornamentation, and yet perfectly free and natural at the same time. Not even the most studied arrangements of the dance exhibit combinations more gracefully and artistically perfect.

Like all young things, kids are extremely inquisitive, and whenever one of them thinks it has made a discovery, the others always immediately determine to find out all about the new subject of interest. In my goat-house there is a hay-rack, placed low enough to be conveniently accessible for the full-grown animals, but rather high for young kids who are supposed to be nurtured on the maternal milk. One of the kids, in the spirit of exploration which characterises them, put its fore-paws against the wall, and got its head level with the bottom of the rack; on which another, desiring to imitate the first, in exactly the same place, could only manage it by getting on his brother's back. The same desire took possession of their sister, who got upon the back of number two. It is evident that only the first of the three could reach the hay, so that the two others remained in a state of unavailing aspiration. They reminded me of the consequence of imitation in literature and the fine arts. An original artist has access for himself to nature, but his imitators think to get at the hay by climbing upon his back, which is just the way *not* to get at it. There is plenty of it to right and left, if they would go to it for themselves.

Sometimes the experiments made by a set of inquisitive kids must of necessity be successive. For example, if there is a basket in the place which will hold one of them, and no more, the others watch him with great interest; and as soon as he jumps out (which he is never very long in doing), the others inevitably jump in and out again by turns. A game of this kind will last till one of the kids has a new suggestion to make, which his brethren are sure to adopt; for they are always very ready in adopting any suggestion which promises a variety in their amusements. It became the fashion one day amongst my kids to carry a little sprig of green between the lips; and a very pretty fashion it was, from a painter's point of view, as it supplied a most refreshing touch of colour amongst the blacks and greys. There is a certain impudence and fearlessness about kids which is often both laughable and charming. One day, whilst I was at work sketching, the kids took it into their heads to try to upset my seat by getting under it, and lifting me up with their not very Samson-like shoulders. This they tried in turn; but, not being powerful enough to succeed, turned their attention to my great dog, who lay by me contemplating their gambols with a sort of half tolerance mingled with disdain. First one kid came up to Tom, and brought his tiny visage in contact with Tom's astonished physiognomy; then another tried the same experiment; and finally, of course, the third tried it. At last the dog's dignity could stand it no longer, and he rushed out of the place, not trusting himself to refrain from using his mighty jaws, which would have crushed a kid's head like a nutshell.

Most young things (young crocodiles and some other reptiles excepted) appear to be reservoirs of pent-up natural energy that finds vent in irrepressible gambols. Of all active young creatures intimately known to me, kids are the most active. When they seem to be perfectly still and reasonable, a spring is touched, and they bound straight up as if the earth had suddenly become elastic and thrown them towards the sky like projectiles. They pass from moods of venturesome and reckless frolic to moods of extreme caution. When in the latter, they studiously examine some object in the place where they are confined, and the boldest of them approaches it first, ready, however, to withdraw upon any appearance of danger. The others follow behind, at regular intervals. In all this they are doing in play what they will have to do in earnest in after-life. The gambols prepare them for the bold leaping amongst rocks and precipices, whilst the *éclaireur* work prepares them for the duty of a prudent sentinel when the wolves are near in the mysterious and deceptive moonlight.

If kids compose beautifully in action, I think they do so still more beautifully in repose. The expression of fraternal trust and affection is strongest, by far, in their moments of perfect rest. They lay their heads upon each other's bodies, as upon pillows, and pass in an instant to the land of innocent dreams; where, no doubt, they play over again, in fancy, the wild gambols that have brought them this sweet weariness. The attitudes of rest are varied beyond all imagination of painter or of poet, and often quaintly original to a degree which no invention could suggest. What they express most commonly is *mutuality*, the interchange of the same offices of kindness and perfect trust. Kids have a way of composing themselves symmetrically in repose as they have in active recreation, so that the designers of classic panels for some sylvan temple or retreat would have little else to do than to copy their natural groupings in order to produce works quite in harmony with the symmetrical classic taste. The heads have an inevitable way of clustering together, and the throat of one kid is always sure to lie across the neck of another. If there are three, the heads often make three steps from the ground upwards; one lying on the ground itself, the other two rising behind it, something like the heads of clerk, curate, and preacher, in an old-fashioned English church.

In conclusion, I should say that kids are typical of two things mainly, innocent gaiety and fraternal affection. One is accustomed to consider them pretty, and no doubt they produce on the mind a complex effect which we call prettiness, but it would be difficult to prove to any one who did not love them that they possessed the attributes of beauty. Few young animals are really beautiful, though most of them are extremely interesting. Beauty appears to have been reserved for the perfected form, whilst the immature form has to be satisfied with a sort of hint of it, or approximation to it. The head of the kid is more beautiful than that of the mature animal, but its body is, in truth, very ungainly. I have never seen this ungainliness more strikingly exemplified than when young kids tried to stand on a waxed floor, as slippery as ice; but this awkwardness has a certain charm, and attaches us to young animals by its expression of weakness, immaturity, and imperfection. Much of the imperfection in the form of kids is compensated for, or disguised by beautiful markings in the colouring of the hair. No animal affords finer studies of black and white, variegated by delicate warm and cold greys. Lines of white are often sharply reserved, especially down each side of the face, and on other parts of the body there are fanciful patches, or soft gradations of a kind often quite as delightful to a painter as the beautiful markings of creatures much more elegantly constructed. And although a kid is decidedly not elegant in form, it is quite as much so as a foal even of the most distinguished race. In both these animals the only really beautiful part is the head, and we accept the rest with a sort of hopeful indulgence, with which is mingled not a little tenderness of affection like that we have for the imperfect language of young children. The heads of kids often remind us of the beautiful heads of deer. There is a sweetness, a refinement about them which disappears later; besides which the head of a kid is more intelligent than that of the mature animal, the forehead is larger in proportion, and the eyes, though not so brilliant and decided in their colouring, are better placed, and have not that vacant expression they often acquire in maturity. The extreme mobility of the ears, which are often extremely beautiful both in shape and texture, and lined with a delicate fur, adds greatly to the liveliness of the expression. Kids have a sharp, wide-awake look, which not unfrequently degenerates into blank stupidity in the mature animal. The same thing may be observed sometimes in the human race; amongst the heavy, stolid races of mankind the children seem more intelligent than their parents, but gradually lose this intelligence (which is mere liveliness) as they grow older, duller, and less easily moved or awakened. It would be easy to criticise the kid's mouth, and if any one chose to affirm that the projections of the lower jaw, and the flattening about the nostrils, were ungraceful, it would be in vain to argue the point; yet in this, as in so many other things, nature produces a pretty and harmonious *whole* by parts which, taken separately, are not absolutely in accordance with our preconceived notions of beauty. I think it might be argued, however, that the delicately cut openings of the nostrils themselves and the sharp line between them, and the projected curve of the lip, are beautiful, at any rate in the best examples.

If you pass from the head to the body you can scarcely fail to admire the fawn-like beauty of the neck, and a fine curve in it often seen from behind. In the mature animal the neck becomes more nearly horizontal, and much less graceful, so that the head is not carried so elegantly, There is a mixture of elegance and pride (if so utterly innocent a creature as a kid could feel anything like pride) in the way it holds its head, especially in the attitude of attention; and much of this is due to the position of the neck, often nearly vertical, with a sharp little curve where it joins the skull, which gives a valuable accent in a drawing. The body has no beauty of form, it is too thin for that; and the legs are mere stilts, as awkward as legs can be; but we forget these deficiencies entirely for the sake of the exquisite *naïveté* which marks every movement of the creature, and which attaches us to it from the first. No one who has the genuine love of animals can resist the attractiveness of kids; and when once you love them their shapelessness is utterly forgotten. You may prove that they are ugly by logic, but you feel that they are lovable and delightful, and by a common confusion you say that they are beautiful. And in the strictest truth they *are* beautiful; not, however, with the beauty which a designer or a sculptor specially cares for, but with that which a painter loves. The goat, in all the stages of his existence, is especially a painter's animal. No creature surpasses him in the pictorial beauty of his hair. For sharp and brilliant contrasts, fine markings, soft gradations, rich varieties of warm and cold greys, the covering of the goat incomparably surpasses that of every other domestic animal, whilst its texture is tempting in the extreme. In kids you have all this beauty with a freshness and newness which is their own. As there is a perfection of unspoiled newness in the thin, rosy, delicately marked skin of a baby's fingers, so the kid possesses a fur quite fresh from the stores of Nature, with the curve of every hair in crisp perfection, exactly in its right place. How snowy the white is! how intensely sable the black! how delicately opportune the sprinkling of badger-like greys! how fine the thin pencillings where the hair is glossy and close! how full and rich the shadowy colour where it is tufted!

I have not space to say much about kids and the poets; but it is clear that the poets have always loved them, and spoken of them tenderly as amongst the most innocent and happy things in the sylvan and pastoral world. The gods loved kids, too, but in a manner which perpetually led to their death on the altar by the hand of some sacrificing priest. How could he bear, I wonder, to see the warm, innocent blood trickling red over the altar's edge? The most innocent things were ever chosen to propitiate the angry gods, and bear the load of human iniquity—not fierce wolves, nor cunning foxes, nor serpents with poisonous fangs, but tender-hearted, faithful doves, and pure white lambs, and playful, fraternal kids.

I think there ought to be, in every house where there are children, some picture or print representing young kids nestling close to each other, their heads reposing on each other, in that sweet peace of their mutual tenderness and trust. We English people have been accused of having weaker fraternal feeling than any other race; and it is said that the feeling, weak as it is already, is becoming feebler still by a gradual atrophy and decline. If this is so, the fact is a melancholy one, and we need a lesson from the kids. Liberty and equality may be unattainable dreams, but we may realise fraternity.

CHAPTER XII.

OTHER ANIMALS.

I INTEND, in this short chapter, to say a few words about the animals of which I know or care least. There are sheep and goats, for instance, of which I know a good deal from long ownership, yet never cared very much; and there are foxes and otters, which would both be very interesting studies, but, as it happens, I never had proper opportunities for studying them. The reader is requested to remember, that in writing these cursory chapters I have never pretended to anything like completeness, but have merely talked in a desultory way about a few familiar creatures that had happened to come within the very limited range of my own personal observation.

A very experienced picture-dealer told me that, so far as his experience went (picture-dealers take note of these things), the most popular of all animals in rustic pictures was the sheep. Rabelais would no doubt have given an explanation of this in his own uncomplimentary way. Rabelais would have said that people like what resembles themselves, and that as mankind are *moutons de Panurge*, they like *moutons* from sympathy and similarity of nature. If it were possible to examine all the people who take pleasure in sheep-pictures, and all the other people who feel indifferent to them, very possibly it might be found that the fondness for sheep was associated with a certain instinct of gregariousness, and that the indifference to them on the other hand prevailed most amongst people who are apt to be somewhat disdainfully self-reliant. I fancy (it may be only a fancy) that there is really some vague association between the disdain of sheep and the spirit of individualism. Let me not be understood to imply that such individualism often leads to disdain of the Divine sherpherding, for no one who considers what men are, and what God must be, can fail to perceive that, relatively to the mysterious and awful Power that made us, we are all incomparably more ignorant and stupid than sheep are relatively to any human pastor. But I do think that this individualism disinclines us to accept the condition of sheepishness in general, and disposes us to rebel against human authorities, and against custom, when they treat us as if we were only fit to be penned, and fleeced, and slaughtered.

Rabelais hit his mark when he noted the close resemblance between men and sheep in the timid following of others. The strongest of us are original only in a few things, in most things we follow the crowd —a sheepishness quite as prevalent in free countries as under despotism. Not that it would be better otherwise; we need this gregariousness for safety and for cohesion, we cannot live in solitude like eagles.

It is not their gregariousness that I dislike in sheep, but their poverty of wit and invention. They belie the promise of their spring. If you had never seen a sheep, and a young lamb were presented to you for the first time, would you not augur well for the future of an animal so charmingly merry and playful? You would say, 'Here is a creature born to learn all things rapidly, since at his second sunrise he is already so much at home upon the earth.' You would not foresee the cloud of dulness which comes on gradually later, like a cataract on the organs of vision, and obscures the narrow brain. Is there anything in nature lovelier than a pasture in early spring, dotted with lambs like snow-patches, and filling the pure air with bleatings? But every day they become less charming and less beautiful, and at last, when fully fleeced, they present scarcely more form than a hedgehog, and the white wool is simply dirty, like linen that has been worn too long. This before shearing—after it they are hideous scarecrows.

After having written these severe things about sheep I feel some twinges of remorse, they are so unpretending, innocent, and submissive. 'As a sheep to the slaughter!' Could any one see the flocks of them driven townwards without pity? From the green pasture, and the summer flowers, and the limpid, alder-shaded rivulet, along the dusty highroad to the streets of the great city, all destined to the inevitable knife, they come in their meekness, unresisting, bringing us food and raiment; and day by day flows the stream of their innocent blood!

In the last chapter I may have become somewhat disproportionately garrulous about kids. I had not so much to say of goats, and deferred it. These creatures certainly decline in intelligence as they approach maturity, and the brain of the full-grown animal is relatively smaller, whilst the skull is inferior in shape. Goats are remarkable for the extreme fidelity with which they follow you; it is not enough to say that they fellow like dogs, they are much closer followers than dogs are. But I doubt if they ever love their masters; it is certain that they reject caresses with the rudest impatience. They are most stupid creatures, and will butt at anything that attracts their attention instead of observing it, as even an ox will in his own dull bovine way. On the other hand, painters may well like goats, because they are by far the most *paintable* of all the rustic animals. They are full of fine texture from horn to hoof, and of good powerful colouring, incomparably superior to the dirty white of sheep, whilst their meagre forms, though not beautiful, are full of sinewy character.

It is to be regretted that a creature so marvellously intelligent as the fox should live, like a clever Bohemian, beyond the pale of society. However, if not an associate of man, he is an object of great respect, almost of positive adoration, and, like other sacred animals, is frequently depicted in the art of the land that pays him homage. I am not aware that the tail of any other creature ever gave any direct spiritual consolation such as a fox's brush may, it appears, afford to a Leicestershire gentleman on his death-bed. Mr. Ruskin mentions a print in which that symbol of the religion of fox-hunting is held before the eyes of a dying Englishman, just as a crucifix is to a Spaniard. Mr. Frank Buckland has a page or two to the same effect. There cannot be any doubt that the fox is a sort of minor deity in some neighbourhoods, and I have personally known men in the West Riding of Yorkshire who worshipped him—to say the least—with a cultus quite as active as that of the Siamese for their white elephants. They certainly believed, in all sincerity, that to shoot a fox was a real sin, and not at all a venial one. They galloped after him three days a-week, the sight of his tail always producing the same unfailing enthusiasm; they talked about him during the other three, and I believe, though I cannot exactly prove it, that they thought of no other deity whilst they sat in the parish church—at least so the Vicar averred, and surely he ought to know. The worship of the fox has produced its own school of fine art; and as Raphael painted Madonnas, and Angelico angels, so many industrious artists have devoted their skill to the illustration of this sacred little quadruped. I cannot, however, add that this religion has been very favourable to the higher interests of art. In the first place, the beast himself is so small in physical dimensions, notwithstanding his enormous moral influence, that he occupies no space on the canvas, whilst the scenery in which he is hunted is from the artistic point of view as uninteresting as scenery well can be. The vestments of his high-priests are dreadful things to paint, and are the despair of genuine artists; not like the beautiful things of nature for any inimitable loveliness, but because they are so glaringly obtrusive and so difficult to unite harmoniously with anything else in creation, except flamingoes and boiled lobsters, which the most ingenious artistic composer can scarcely find a pretext for introducing. Seriously, all pictures and coloured prints of fox-hunting, however much talent and skill may be lavished upon them, are excluded from the category of fine art by the very nature of the subject, and it is a pity that the ability which is often lavished upon them should be so wasted. They may, of course, be very clever in their way; they often are so; but it is simply impossible to make them harmonies of composed colour. And even the engravings from them cannot be truly artistic, for the costume has a sort of neatness, which, though charming on a tailor's pattern-card, and quite in harmony with the generally tidy look of our civilisation in saddlery and harness, in carriage-building, boat-building, and the rest, is neither picturesque like romantic costume nor pure like the nudities or draperies of the Greeks. A well-dressed gentleman in top-boots going neatly over a stiff fence on a very well-bred horse, is a pretty example of the results of discipline, but does not afford material for a picture. In fact, it is a sort of material to be best dealt with by some kindly and intelligent caricaturist like John Leech, whose hunting-scenes have much more truth and life than the pictures of more ambitious artists, whilst they are artistic exactly to the degree which the subject naturally calls for.

By far the most picturesque hunting which is to be seen in England is otter-hunting. It always leads you along the banks of some stream which is sure to be rich in itself, and which gains much by the presence of animated and interested people, who forget to be stiff and shy in their eagerness about the hunt, and whose costume harmonises agreeably with the greys and browns of nature. If, however, there is one thing more to my taste than following an otter when he is hunted, it is to get a quiet look at him when his mind is perfectly at ease. There are otters in the stream behind my house, but no regular otter-hounds in the neighbourhood; nor should I regret the absence of them, were it not that otters are so destructive of fish, killing not for hunger merely, but for sport. I had an opportunity not long since of watching an otter under rather peculiar circumstances, as to effect. It was late evening, and I was walking with my dog near the river-side, on its eastern bank, the dog being nearer the water than I was. There still remained a glow in the west, but all the landscape was in the obscurity of advanced twilight, so that it was very difficult to distinguish anything. Suddenly, my dog began to bark in an extraordinary manner, as if some wild animal were before him, and on prostrating myself so as to get the river bank against the light reflection from the western sky, I at once beheld a very fine otter in perfect black *silhouette* against the still brilliant water. He hesitated a few seconds, then dashed into the stream and escaped. This is just the way I like to pursue wild animals—to watch them quietly in their own haunts, not to slaughter or wound them. When sportsmen lose their tempers because some poor quadruped has had speed and cleverness enough to save itself I am always secretly delighted, but of course dare not say so openly, for sportsmen are so bloodthirsty that they might become dangerous if too rashly contradicted.

Many years ago there was a tame otter in my neighbourhood, which showed great attachment for its human friends, and had a playful disposition. It would come when called, like a dog, and behaved in every respect like a trustworthy household pet. This otter behaved perfectly in the dining-room, and ate of everything except cooked fish. It is curious that in this instance the hereditary taste did not show itself in the refusal of strange kinds of food, but in a connoisseur's fastidiousness about the one aliment on which the creature's ancestors had fed. It refused all fish that was not both raw and perfectly fresh. The only other hereditary peculiarity worth mentioning was the necessity for frequently plunging its head and fore-limbs in water, and to satisfy this need a bucket was regularly provided. Curiously enough, when taken to the river-side, this otter did not willingly swim, but if left to itself would merely use the river-brink as its bucket. This is the more strange when we consider that the structure of the otter is so admirably adapted for swimming, since all his feet are webbed, and he can propel himself in water with great rapidity.

CHAPTER XIII.

BIRDS.

I BELIEVE that every human being, however situated in the world of reality, however little given to flights of imagination, has at one time or other dreamed that he was endowed with wings, and skimming with prodigious rapidity at a safe elevation above the irregular surfaces of the globe. I feel quite assured beforehand, that every reader of these chapters, even if he happens to live at an immense distance from the writer of them, or a century after the said writer shall be dead and buried, will be more or less in the habit of flying in his dreams.

I have directly asked not a few grave gentlemen and ladies whether *they* flew in this manner, and they have invariably answered that they did. Sometimes we fly to escape some terrible danger; enemies crowd round us, and just when they become most menacing we suddenly remember that nature has provided us with the means of safety: we give a stroke or two with our mighty pinions, and swiftly raise ourselves beyond the reach of our tormentors. At other times we are flying on a great journey: cities, fields, forests, pass under us, and then the green land comes to an end, and the blue ocean rolls below, sprinkled with white-sailed ships. It may be observed, that when any one dreams that he is flying, that accomplishment is always a personal accomplishment of his own, giving him a remarkable superiority over others. If he is in love, he holds out a hand to the beloved one and says, 'Let us fly away together!' but he never imagines that common humanity can do anything but walk slowly about upon the earth and gaze at him wonderingly with upturned faces.

These vain and idle dreams are a reflection of man's ancient envy and baffled aspiration. Men have always wished that they could fly, and have always felt a little hurt by the superiority of so many inferior creatures in the matter of locomotion. For nobody affects to deny that of all the varieties of locomotion flying is quite incomparably the most perfect. It is by far the swiftest, to begin with; though, since men use express trains, birds are not so superior as they used to be in the matter of simple rapidity. The one splendid superiority of flying is, that from any one point of the earth's surface to any other point the road is straight as a ray of light and perfect as polished ice, that it never needs repair, that it invades no one's property, and has to pay no rents nor compensations. The great 'highway of nations,' the ocean of salt water, has some of these advantages also, but in a degree how inferior! The ship meets a sand-bank and is arrested, the waves break over her and she becomes a wreck. The bird meets a mountain and rises over it, nor can any barrier of rock or fortification arrest her. Think of the difference between a ship sailing to India round by the Cape of Good Hope, or even, if you will, by the costly new canal at Suez, and a bird flying to India over land and sea! Yes, the great ocean of water, glorious as it is, may not be compared with the still vaster ocean of the air, the shoreless ocean, so thin and clear, that submerges all the hills and valleys of the world, and in which not even the loftiest Alp was ever islanded! We are grovelling at the bottom of it, like starfish in the mud of the Atlantic; but the birds are its swift fishes, having wings for fins, and they alone have the freedom of the blue that is above us!

We may well dream about that marvellous faculty of flight; poets may well imagine that if they knew its secrets and had experienced its unimaginable sensations, they would write more glorious verse. Did you ever, reader, fairly and seriously set yourself to realise what flying would be like, supposing of course (as we always *do* suppose) that you retained your human feelings, your human capacity for intellectual enjoyment of the scenes that passed before you? I have sometimes so fixed my thoughts upon these imaginations, that at last, by a reaction of the wearied fancy, I landed in a strange scepticism about all flying. Could it be possible that any creatures sustained themselves in the air, and propelled themselves with the rapidity of an express train, by means of feathers fastened to skin and agitated by muscles? There are times in the depth of the night when these doubts will visit the sleepless pillow, just as we doubt sometimes whether there can be such realities as the battle of Sadowa or the siege of Paris; but the morning comes and we resume our dull acquiescence in the facts, neither doubting them nor realising them. The swallows fly about the house; have not swallows flown about it ever since we were born, in these months of May and June? Is not flying common enough, and what sensible person would trouble his mind about what can be seen every day and every where?

To realise what flying is, we need to deliver ourselves from the effects of this familiarity and to recover the faculty of wonder. For however common and familiar flying may be, it is of all the Divine inventions one of the most marvellous. The extreme marvellousness of it is sufficiently proved by the fact that all our men of science cannot imitate it, though the models exist in the greatest variety and abundance, and they have nothing to do but copy. No human being really proposes to himself to *invent* a flying-machine: the machine is already invented and in the fullest perfection: all that men have to do is to copy it, and this they cannot achieve for want of a material having the strength of bird-muscle, in combination with its lightness and power of contraction. When you carve a grouse or a woodcock, or any wild bird that flies, you sever in the flesh of the breast a marvel which belongs as yet exclusively to nature. Men can make steam-engines and watches, but they cannot make light muscle, with its tremendous power of contraction; and they cannot make anything combining its lightness with its active strength. It is this combination of lightness with strength and resistance to wear and tear, which always marks the superiority of mechanical artificers. A cart built in a village may be as strong as a carriage from Long Acre; but then, how heavy it is! The clumsiest boat-builder can make a boat, but not a light one like Clasper or Searle. And when the object of Nature is to produce a creature uniting lightness and strength, she goes so much beyond all human artificers in this difficult combination that they cannot follow her, even at a distance. A balloon *floats* in the air. Nature alone makes things that will *swim* in the air. Now the difference in marvellousness between aquatic and aerial swimming may be estimated with perfect exactness, since it depends upon the difference of gravity in the two fluids. The weight of air displaced by even a large bird is so minute, that we may practically consider him as a creature sustained in the air entirely by his own exertions. M. Michelet, in one of those amazingly unscientific passages which often stagger us in the midst of his prose-poetry, said that birds floated, and could make themselves lighter than air by swelling themselves at will.* It is useless to waste space in demonstrating the absurdity of this, for the reader who does not see it on the instant would be unable

---

* 'Il enfle son volume, donc diminue sa pesanteur relative; dès lors il monte de lui-même *dans un milieu plus lourd que lui.—L'Oiseau*, 6th edition, p. 28.

to follow the demonstration. The truth is, that under all circumstances, and whether puffed up or not, every bird that flies is so much heavier than air, that he is never aided by any floating power, or buoyancy, whatever. He maintains himself solely by the effort of his wings, and how prodigious that effort must be, relatively to the creature's weight, every swimmer knows. Men swim in a medium so dense that many human bodies can float in it without an effort, and yet the little labour that is needed to keep the head above the surface and ensure a slow advance is enough to produce rapid exhaustion, even in the most robust. If we think of flight as a kind of swiming which it is, the marvel of it will be much more plain to us. Think how long these swimmers of the air-ocean can continue without rest! It is not so much their prodigious speed which surprises, for in a medium offering so little resistance as the air it is natural that creatures should travel swiftly, if they can travel at all; that which is really astonishing is their sustained energy, a superiority to fatigue resembling rather the divine force of gods and angels than the efforts of mortal weariness. To live on the wing like the swallow, to traverse oceans like the albatross, a creature must have wells of inward energy like those deep mysterious fountains which have never been known to fail.

What the bird thinks and feels, what flying is to *him*, we know not. Some people will tell us that the gladness which poets have attributed to him is imaginary, and that in reality the sublime flights the poet sings of are to the bird himself no more than a perfectly prosaic way of getting his living and making unavoidable journeys. But is there not reason to believe, even in an inquiry so difficult as this, that we may obtain a little light from our human experience? Do we not invariably rejoice in the possession of our own physical faculties, when they are perfect enough to be capable of sustained activity, without any unpleasant reaction afterwards? It is needless to put such a question as this to the active English race. We delight in all the varieties of motion that are possible for us—in riding, rowing, swimming, skating, even in the prosaic exercise of pedestrianism. And this delight is certainly not the result of reason in our race, or of reaction from intellectual labour, for it is strongest in the young who never reason about anything, and in adults belonging to the classes which do hardly any intellectual work. It is a purely physical pleasure, combining the sense of relief from the uneasiness of inaction with the enjoyment of an agreeable stimulus. Now the more finely-organised of the lower animals are just as capable of enjoying physical pleasures as we are. When your dog goes out with you he does twenty miles to your five, yet you do not order him to run the superfluous fifteen: he runs them because he rejoices in the exercise. A horse that seems exhausted when just taken out of harness will gallop wildly round the pasture with his comrades. Who forces him to gallop? He is not spurred by spiked balls, like the maddened racers in the Roman corso. If quadrupeds delight in the free use of their terrestrial swiftness, so may the birds fly gladly in their play-heaven of infinite air. And I have no doubt that every healthy bird flies quite as much because he likes it, as with any definite purpose of providing for his family. In the life of all wild creatures there is no rigid demarcation between duty and amusement: they do not divide action under separate moral heads; they fulfil what we call duties (such as building habitations and providing for their families), but always pleasurably, as a grouse-shooter or salmon-fisher increases the supplies of his larder.

If the reader never studied birds on the wing he may be glad to know how it can be conveniently done. With a rather powerful telescope, so fixed on a tripod as to be rapidly movable in every direction, you may follow the flight of many kinds of birds without losing sight of them for an instant, and observe at the same time many refinements of motion which at that distance would escape the naked eye. Flying is as delicate an art as the most perfect skating or rowing, and many a wild bird is an artist in his way, delighting in the exercise of his skill. To every one who takes pleasure in seeing perfectly accomplished action, such as perfect rowing, or dancing, or horsemanship, let me recommend the study of a kestrel with a telescope as he slowly circles with motionless wings, or hangs exactly in the same place, though the wind may be rushing past him at the rate of twenty miles an hour. At times he alters slightly the angle of his wings, and now and then they quiver, but the precise sufficiency of the change to answer the alterations of the aerial currents is proved by the fixity of the bird. Of all the varieties of flight to be easily observed in England that of the kestrel is the most beautiful; and if the bird's art, in its origin divine and improved by the practice of unnumbered generations, were not far above the gropings of human science, it might be added that it is the most scientific. The kestrel wastes no effort, he sets his wings as if he had studied the decomposition of forces, and the powers of the air support him. The eagle has the same science, but of him I say little, having rarely seen him wild. Macgillivray tells us that most eagles and hawks have the habit of sailing or floating in circles, 'as if for amusement.'

It may be observed that the importance of birds in pictorial art and in sculpture bears a very irregular relation to their importance in natural history, and even in poetry. Several birds are eagerly sought by naturalists which the artist seldom concerns himself about, either on account of their extreme rarity and the consequent inconvenience of study, or else because they are too insignificant in appearance. Poets never weary of the nightingale, but painters wisely avoid the inimitable songstress. If some artist attempted to illustrate the exquisite opening of *Parisina* :—

> 'It is the hour when from the boughs
> The nightingale's high voice is heard,'

we know the sort of illustration that might be expected. He would give us an evening landscape, with foliage against the clearness of the sky, and then, somewhere on the extremity of a twig, a dickeybird of some kind, supposed to be a nightingale but much exaggerated in size, would reward the investigations of the persevering student. The nightingale, reversing the great lesson of our infancy, is heard and not seen; poets may praise his singing, and violinists may imitate it if they can, but painters have nothing to do with him. How he fills the woods at midnight! Invisible, hidden for the greater majesty of the effect, he, no larger than one of the hundred million leaves, makes them all vibrate to his melody. He, and the skylark, are the beloved birds of poets; but painters like the eagle, the swan, the splendid peacock, the ashy heron, the scarlet ibis. In sculpture, the material goes far to settle the preference; the workers in marble may give us severe abstracts of the terrible bird of Jove, but they wisely avoid all slender stilts and bills. On the other hand, our clever modern wood-carvers, who study nature like painters, take a pride in proving the adaptability of their material, and carve dead snipes and woodcocks, or slender fishers and waders. Precious indeed to the carver are the beautiful forms of birds! Nothing in all the realm of nature has curves of that particular kind of loveliness,—curves so bold and pure, yet restrained by such perfect temperance. Who can tell what Christian art may have gained from one bird emblem, what recondite lessons of beauty were taught by the mystic dove? Age after age the carvers and painters studied him, and learned of him more and more.

CHAPTER XIV.

BIRDS (*continued*).

ONLY the tame birds favour us with the quiet enjoyment of their beauty, for though a quick observer may catch glimpses of the wild ones, and see enough for the purposes of the naturalist, he can seldom study them as artists like to study. For this reason I say less of birds in these chapters than the interest of the subject deserves, not being willing to speak of what I have not seen in nature. There exist, it is true, many poor prisoners in public gardens and private cages, and great quantities of stuffed skins in the glass cases of museums; but in reference to this material I ask myself what relation all this bird-beauty bears to the beauty of the world as man sees it; and the answer is, that for man the world is but little adorned by the beauty of any birds that he has not domesticated. Writing then simply from the human point of view, I find the vast materials of science for the most part unavailable. What do we really see of birds in nature? Usually either specks in the distance or a confusion of rapid movement nearer hand, the form in both cases eluding us. Many of us have seen wild eagles, that is, a pair of dots near the brow of some Highland mountain, which when most visible we should have taken for hawks without the assurance of our guide or gamekeeper. And even much commoner birds than these perpetually elude our sight by the mere rapidity of their motion. Take, for instance, the king-fisher. You are idling by the riverside in summer, and between brown water and green boughs goes a sudden cerulean flash! A zigzag lightning of flaming azure remains for an instant upon the retina, and you know that a king-fisher has passed. But, pray, what have you perceived of his form? What a difference between birds and flowers! how easy it is to see the flowers, that final decoration of the earth; how difficult to watch the birds! Sometimes, when flowers were destroyed in heedlessness, I have wished that they had wings and could escape, but oftener I have desired some magic spell that might fix the bird upon the bough, just till he could be painted! We all know the *Sultana of the Nightingale*—

> 'The maid for whom his melody
> His thousand songs are heard on high
>   .   .   .   .
> His queen, the garden queen, his Rose,'

but how few of us know her lover! And even if birds would let themselves be better seen, it is not in our northern climate that we can estimate their value as a part of the splendour of the world. In the forests of the tropics they are great and gorgeous, clothed with scarlet and green, and the most dazzling orange, and azure as from heaven, and purple of the sea, and crimson of tropical sunsets. In those lands the birds carry the most intense colour everywhere, and must perforce be seen, like a D.C.L. in his academical robes, or young Oliver Goldsmith in his scarlet breeches. But of our northern birds, though many of them have pretty and rather bright colours, when you examine them, the prevailing impression is conveyed by the adjective so frequently used by Mr. Morris in his poetry, when he talks simply of 'the brown bird.' They delight the ear rather than the eye, and as a visible part of our northern nature their position is modest in the extreme. The sea-birds show best of all, flashing white on green wave and azure sky, and so repeating the brilliant accents of the foam-flake and the cloud. The common sea-gull, though he boasts no charm of voice, holds a far more important rank in pictorial nature than the nightingale or the lark. And there are places on the wild coasts where the sea-fowl can no more be omitted by the painter than mankind in the streets of cities. *Their* cities are the inaccessible cliffs whose grandeur gains enormously by their tumultuous clouds of wings. No mist-wreath on alpine precipice has the majesty of those unnumbered multitudes; no song in southern woodland has the poetry of their discordant cries. Behind them the iron-bound coast where their nests are made; below them—a thousand feet below them—the restless, pitiless breakers that cast the wreck against the rock; in front of them the unquiet plain of waters, storm-swept, inhospitable, without one friendly bough, or any sheltering eaves! Truly these creatures have a stern and drear existence, and there is a watchful gravity in their aspect altogether different from the light-headedness of the sylvan songsters. They are not happy as chirping sparrows are happy, but have something of the ocean's melancholy, and the grave bearing of hard-living fishermen, the toilers of the sea.

Sea-gulls are beautiful when the sky is clear and blue, and the bright sunshine brings out the purity of their forms, yet I like them better against darkly-lowering clouds, and best of all when the black tempest is brewing, and they have their part in the increasing anxiety and agitation of nature. At such a time as that, when the watchful mariner reefs his sails, and looks to every rope and spar with redoubled caution, the gulls are blown across the darkening heaven, and the floating divers are tossed on the rising waves. Then the little petrel runs down the trough of the sea, and the sailor inwardly prayeth. These wild birds are safer than he is; they can rest on their wings like a balloon in the tranquil heart of the hurricane. Only when they touch the water need they know that a storm is raging.

I think, of all the travelling that is done upon the planet, the travelling of some great sea-bird, such as the albatross for instance, is the most sublime. Think of him leaving some barren rock in the Austral Ocean, and without further preparation than the unfolding of his mighty wings, setting forth on a voyage of two or three hundred leagues! The qualities of self-reliance and self-help, which we are told that we ought to acquire, belong much more decidedly to the albatross than to any human being who ever existed. The truth is, that not 'self-help,' but 'mutual help' must be the motto of humanity, and it is only by association that we travel. Even our brave Livingstone, one of the most self-reliant travellers ever known, needs the help of many negroes for the accomplishment of his designs; and we know with what an imposing force the great Pasha, Sir Samuel Baker, has lately gone southwards from the land of Egypt to the sources of the Nile. Merely to be in a modern steamship is in fact to accept the services of a thousand laborious human helpers, but when the albatross sails forth alone nothing but the natural forces aid him; he propels himself by his own unwearied pinions, and seeks his food in the waves below. Self-reliance of that genuine kind is quite beyond us, our human self-reliance being simply the confidence in our power of getting money, on which we really rely, and which means the help of all humanity. The great lonely birds *are* self-reliant, and what a noble absence of fear is needed for the daily habit of their lives! Man's nervous apprehension of possible evil would hinder his use of their powers if he possessed them. If we could fly to America we should want floating dining-rooms under us for refreshment, and hospitals in case of sickness or fatigue.

It seems as if it would be pleasanter to be one of the

gregarious birds than one of the solitaries, but the help we most value, that given to us in weakness or disease, is denied to the ailing members of a flock of birds, who must keep the regulated pace. In this respect the tame swan is more fortunate than his ancestors, since his life, though less active, is more tranquil and independent. The difference is very exactly that between an officer *en retraite*, and the soldier under the flag. The discipline of the wild gregarious birds is very regular and severe, and they are all the stronger and more active for this discipline. Domestication is always, in a certain sense, deterioration. Birds may grow larger in the domestic state, they may weigh more, and a couple of them may make a more sufficient dinner, when they are bred specially for the table, but the living creature is not what he was. The true degradation of the bird is to lose the power of flight. Our tame swans are very beautiful; they have a developed luxurious beauty like that of garden flowers, of enormous lilies and roses, but *can they fly?* Beautiful as are the swans upon the Thames, admirably as they adorn the rich reaches of a landscape which without them would be all but perfect, and with them is the ideal realised, what, after all, does the Londoner know of swans? He alone who has heard at once the harmony of their hundred wings, and seen the white flock come to earth on the borders of some lonely mere, he alone knows the tribe or nation of the swans! 'There is a wild harmony,' says Charles St. John, 'in their bugle-cry as they wheel round and round, now separating into small companies as each family of five or six seems inclined to alight; and now all joining again in along undulating line, waiting for the word of command of some old leader!' You may see this occasionally in the remote Highlands, or more frequently you may hear the sounds of wings far above you in the night—the 'gabble raches' or 'gabriel ratchets' of popular superstition, the passing of the aerial hunter with all his noisy hounds!

Still, if the swan that is commonly known to us has not this collective grandeur, he has even superior individual beauty. The wild swan is not so beautiful, nor so majestic, as the living ornament of our own familiar Thames. No painter who undertook to represent a royal progress on the river would fail to give us the noble bird close to the royal barge. His white breast meets the wavelets, impelled invisibly by rhythmic impulses, his soft wings catch the gentle airs of summer, whilst high on the graceful neck dwells the living head that governs that perfect motion! What need of green of parrot, or scarlet of flamingo, or insect iridescence? What need of any colour but that effulgent whiteness, that golden beak, and that one touch of black?

We have full liberty to enjoy the beauty of these glorious birds without any prosaic drawback from our ideal. They are completely and harmoniously majestic. They are full of courage, they are devotedly faithful and affectionate, and they live a hundred years. Yet, since the bird who could match the eagle in courage and man himself in longevity, and with whose beauty the king of the gods did not disdain to clothe himself, had never given the least sign of any musical talent or accomplishment; the fertile human imagination, always so unwilling to leave any hiatus in its ideals, invented that most poetical fable of the swan's song at the close of a songless life; as if the bird which had never been musical when most happy, became so in the dark shadow of imminent dissolution. Of all strange old beliefs, I think this is one of the most curiously beautiful. Our forefathers took it quite seriously, and went and listened for the melody of dying swans, as the Queen of Navarre went to see a young lady die, that she might catch a glimpse of the soul as it passed between the body and the ceiling. The same Queen of Navarre explained the swan's song by the supposition that the bird's spirit, leaving the body through so long a neck, would produce musical murmurs. Michelet half believes that the swan really did sing in Virgil's time, but that since then, having come into northern climes, her Muse, which was of the south, is mute, and the bird alone survives.

With all our delight in art, and our interest in natural history, it may be doubted whether we care for bird-beauty so much as they did in the middle ages. We are certainly not so fond of having peacocks in our gardens as our ancestors were, and their greater appreciation of the peacock is still more clearly proved by their custom of serving him at high festivals with all his most magnificent plumage. They wore, too, the plumes of birds, as the most perfect top or finial of costume. In Japanese art, which up to the present date corresponds accurately to our art of the Middle Ages, birds have an important place and are treated with remarkable power and knowledge. The truth is, that to admire birds quite heartily and sufficiently it appears as if a little childishness were necessary. All children take an interest in birds, as all properly constituted women do in flowers, and our best impressions of birds are, I believe, not really recent, but reminiscences of very early youth. I distinctly remember that a lady who had a peacock gave me one of its most splendid feathers, at a time when neither literature nor art could have taught any appreciation of beauty; but the intensity of that colour, the gleaming splendour of those filaments are distinct in my memory yet. The business-like gravity of this nineteenth century prevents all serious persons of the male sex from putting feathers in their hats (except a few picturesque Volunteers); yet surely there is something excessive in our disdain of these, the most perfect of all ornaments, which the dying birds bequeath. Nothing in nature is more beautiful than a feather, with its delicate tapering curves, and colour always admirable in its way, whether the prevailing note of it be one of sobriety or of splendour. The savage who covers his whole mantle with short feathers closely arranged as on a dove's breast, proves his sensibility to a kind of natural beauty which civilised men neglect. Even our English birds supply a very complete scale of colour, and if not rich in the brilliant contrasts of the tropics, they are often admirable for those delicate gradations and quiet harmonies which the cultivated eye prefers. The varieties of grey and brown in sea-fowl and mountain-game correspond to the rich varieties of the same colour-motives in rainy skies and autumnal or wintry landscape, and the more we come to know of colour the more alive we are to these less obvious beauties.

Were it not that space is failing me I should like to speak at length about the birds we have domesticated. Of these the pigeons are the most beautiful, and the favourites of poets and painters. They look their best in the intense sunshine of a southern summer, wheeling round some mediæval dovecote tower, with the dark blue sky behind them. The white ones are my favourites, on account of their dazzling purity, and the completeness with which their whole form is revealed, as if it were carved in marble; but the details of colouring in other varieties are often very interesting when you see them near at hand; and several excellent painters (need I name John Lewis?) have studied their wonderful blues and purples with the care and diligence which they deserve. Still more frequently painted are our familiar acquaintances of the poultry-yard, Chanticleer the splendid and the proud, with all his humble harem. Painters find in them a mine of rich warm colour and plenty of characteristic attitude, and poultry have been so associated with human life from very remote antiquity, that they have quite an important place in literature. Without wishing to detract from the merits of any other artist, I may allude, in passing, to the admirable poultry of

Charles Jacque, who, so far as my knowledge goes, has drawn them better than anybody else, as to the truth and variety of attitude and expression. He has, to begin with, the gifts of the born animal-painter, and is a great poultry-fancier also, which has no doubt much strengthened his habits of observation. His countryman, M. Bracquemond, is especially strong in water-fowl, and few subjects of a familiar kind are more rewarding to an artist of real ability. There is a great deal of beautiful colour about ducks, from the rich soft gold of the fluffy ducklings, to the deep iridescence of a drake's neck, and the strong markings on his wings, besides which the painter of water-fowl gets the ripples and reflections of the liquid surface, which are better worth painting than the trodden straw of the farm-yard.

I leave the hens and ducks somewhat hastily and reluctantly, in order to have space for a few words about the manner in which birds are usually treated. Instead of finding a tranquil pleasure in watching the habits of these most admirable and interesting creatures, the average European thinks only about shooting them. If a boy happens to discover a heron by the side of some quiet stream, the one idea that instantly takes possession of his mind is the regret that he has no gun; and if, unfortunately, the weapon happens to be in his hands, he kills the heron (or more probably wounds him) without a moment's doubt or hesitation. When the boy becomes a man, the passion for killing has strengthened into a confirmed habit, made inveterate by the pride of skill.

The wild bird is not looked upon as a creature to be treated with more hospitality than a wolf; everybody fires at him as at some noxious vermin. Even the scientific naturalist adds yearly to the long catalogue of destruction, to supply his dissecting-room with bodies and his glass cases with stuffed skins. And so it comes to pass that the wild birds of civilised countries are every year more rare, and we are all as ignorant about them as people must be who have nothing but books of science, without that personal familiarity which alone makes knowledge alive. The late Mr. Waterton, the naturalist, gave a fine example in his gentle hospitality. Round his house in Yorkshire was a great space of land, with wood and water, encircled by a protecting wall; within that space no gun was ever fired, it was the guarded paradise of the birds. In their assurance of perfect peace they did not shun man's friendly observation. Without our stupid destructiveness there might be many such bird-Edens as that. The birds do not avoid us naturally. It has always been noted by voyagers that in lands hitherto uninhabited and unvisited by man they sat quietly within gunshot, looking at their strange visitors with undismayed curiosity. If men had treated them kindly they might have been our friends. Did the reader ever happen to meet with the well-known birds' friend in the garden of the Tuileries,—an old man whose life had been saddened by the loss of those he loved, and who sought consolation in his solitude, and found it in the friendship of little birds? They flew about his head, not as the bird in Rubens's picture of his sons, which is held by a piece of string, but bound by no thread except the invisible one of their gratitude, and affection, and expectation. Not entirely disinterested or unselfish in their love, yet was it full of trust, and that trust quite a personal and peculiar one, for it was given to him alone. A minute before he came into the garden they were wild birds still, and when he had gone home they returned to their lofty trees; but whilst he walked there in the afternoon they went and talked with him as if he had been their father, settling on his shoulders and his arms, and picking the crumbs close to his careful feet. They must have wondered at his absence when he died, and even now, though things are so changed since then, and the Palace is a blackened ruin, and it seems as if centuries had passed, I believe that those little sparrows and finches still remember their old friend, and would make a fluttering cloud of gladness about his head if he could come from the cemetery where he sleeps and revisit the chestnut shades.

The practice of keeping these sweet singers in cages is of all cruelties the most pardonable, for it proceeds from love alone, and yet I may enter here a not intemperate protest. The truth is, that of caged birds and their happiness or unhappiness I am simply and absolutely ignorant, never having permitted that kind of imprisonment where I had any power to prevent it. In this matter the practice of Leonardo da Vinci seems the best for us to imitate; for though he did indeed purchase little singing-birds in cages, it was only to set them free.

Ah! that first taste of recovered liberty, when the wings beat no longer against the pitiless wires but flew in the boundless air! Had they known, those ransomed wanderers, that their liberator had bought their freedom, would they not have come back to him every day to fill his garden with their songs, and tell him the secret of their nests in the depths of the distant woods?

In the same spirit of kindness the Norwegian peasants put a sheaf of unthreshed wheat on the roof of the house at Christmas. Soon the news of this rare feast spreads far and wide amongst the half-starved birds in the forest, and they come like a swarm of bees. Is not that better than attracting larks* by the flashes of a treacherous mirror, and shooting them from an ambush?

* I wish all song-birds were rank poison,—there might be some chance of preserving them then. What right-minded person can eat larks and thrushes without compunction? One of the most odious and monstrous sights to be met with in Europe is a fat and vulgar French bagman devouring a dish of sky-larks. Look at him as he eats, not inaudibly, and think of Shelley's verse! Only imagine those abominable old Romans who swallowed platefuls of nightingales' tongues! How perfectly *bête* was their notion of luxury! how stupid to fancy that because the nightingale sang so sweetly her tongue must be particularly succulent! It would be as reasonable to make a dish of old fiddle-strings.

•

CHAPTER XV.

ANIMALS IN ART.

SOME years ago, wandering in Picardy, I stayed for the night at a certain inn, and having ordered some beef for supper, had the satisfaction of seeing a whole ox placed on the table before me. The *garçon* of the establishment, who was also the cook, gave me indeed the dish my hunger craved for after a walk of twenty miles; but by way of a poetical or artistic effect (which could have occurred to nobody but a Frenchman), he placed at the same time on the table the waxen image of an ox. He set this beast, which was exactly the size of those oxen which Gulliver devoured in Lilliput, on the white tablecloth in front of me, stepped back to look at him as an artist looks at the picture on his easel, then snatched him up hastily, and gave a push to one of the legs and a twist to the tail, replaced him on the table, smiled in conscious triumph and exclaimed, 'There, sir, isn't he perfect?'

He had made this masterpiece whilst engaged in the still more useful and admirable art of cooking the natural beef. There was no denying the cleverness of the performance; the ox was full of life, his attitude expressed a puzzled bovine apprehension as if some alarming little animal were teasing him, every limb was ready for action, and even the eye, though it was merely a hole bored with one of the prongs of a steel fork, seemed to glare with fiery excitement in the dark shadow cast by the lamp. My solitary meal was greatly enlivened by this interesting study, but the artist had still another surprise in reserve. When he entered with the dessert he lifted daintily from a plate of *petits fours* a most savage-looking little wax dog, which being placed in front of the excited ox began, as it seemed, to bark most furiously. He had made the dog whilst looking after those other dishes whose merits had just been very gratefully appreciated.

It is needless to add that we became great friends at once, and that I spent hours with him in the kitchen watching the simultaneous exercise of his two arts. The cookery was never neglected; but whenever the pans could be left to themselves for a minute, the skilful fingers took up the shapeless wax, and pushed and squeezed it into the semblance of some living animal. The man had never studied from nature, except by momentary observation of such living creatures as happened to come in his way, and he had not the most rudimentary notion of the art of drawing; but he had such an instinctive perception of animal life and action, so sure a memory for movement, for everything that goes to the expression of character, that his work was always animated and delightful. The want of systematic study was evident, but not evident at the first glance; his intelligence and sympathy threw dust in the eyes of criticism, and it was only after the first wonder had passed away that one perceived the absence of refinement in the forms and the simple ignorance of art. His history was briefly this. As a child he had lived in the country, and been set to watch pigs; so he had begun, in childhood, to make models of his pigs in clay, since which time modelling had been to him a habit, and his fingers were never quite happy when doing anything else. He had spent a year or two in Paris, terribly overworked at a restaurant on the boulevards, yet even there he had gone on making his little waxen animals. Some famous artists had seen them and had been struck by the surprising natural gift which made them suggest an artistic education; but the lad preferred, perhaps wisely, the modest certainties of his own position, and remained an amateur, full of inborn cleverness, but devoid of science. I gave him a commission to the munificent amount of thirty francs, in return for which he sent me a herd of seventeen animals, all of which are remarkable artistic curiosities, showing what the natural gift may accomplish without the aids of culture.

Now this case is interesting for the light it throws on the nature of that instinct which is the fundamental endowment of the *animalier*. That endowment is the faculty of retaining a characteristic movement, so instantaneous in the living creature that it can never be studied from life. It may be *caught*, it cannot be studied. A man who has this gift of suddenly seizing and permanently retaining the movements which are the most expressive language of animals, holds the art of animal-painting or animal-sculpture by the middle, and the rest may be got by the study of drawing and anatomy; but without that peculiar gift, and it is rare indeed, the most painstaking study is not of the least use. It may even be added, that the finest artistic gifts will fail of their effect if this be wanting. It is certainly, from the purely artistic point of view, a far higher thing to be able to colour beautifully and compose well than to remember quite accurately how a pig looks at you, or how a dog scratches his way into a rat-hole; but the colour of Titian and the composition of Raphael would not have made such an animal-painter as Landseer. The most scientific draughtsmen in Europe could not, with all their science, teach the most docile pupil how to draw such a thing as that hare by Bracquemond in the 'PORTFOLIO,' and you may be a member of the Royal Academy or a *Grand Prix de Rome* without being able to sketch a cat or a squirrel.

This is one of those truths about art which the outside public feels more than artists and critics. Suppose the case of an admirable painter, able to draw well, and colour well, and compose well, but without any special faculty for retaining the expression of animals—suppose that this painter sent animal pictures to the exhibitions, is it not certain that they would be received with coldness in comparison to works having the qualities of

Landseer, and his deficiencies? Every one who knows enough about art to be able to distinguish between the sources of his satisfaction, is aware that although Landseer most deservedly holds splendid and even supreme rank as an *animalier*, and although his painting is a technical wonder, he is not either a colourist or a composer, and that considered simply as painting, notwithstanding the technical and manual marvellousness just alluded to, his art is not of a high order, does not even take rank with the better sort of serious contemporary work. Most of us are fully aware of all this, and yet who begrudges Sir Edwin his splendid rewards in wealth and honour, the popular applause, the royal favour? Do we not all feel that the divine gift which is in him, the gift of placing on canvas the life of an animal, not its body merely as others do, but its feelings and its thoughts, and that with a vividness unrivalled by mortal hand—do we not feel that this gift is to an animal-painter the first and most essential of his talents, and that if outside of it the artist is simply respectable, we need ask from him no more?

It is often believed that animal design is easier than the human figure, and it is true, no doubt, that the *animalier* has a certain latitude which resembles in kind, but not in degree, the latitude of the landscape-painter. If you are painting a sheep, for instance, you need not be particular about individuality, because people in general observe sheep so little that they would not appreciate portraiture; if your sheep have the right sheepish look, and a shape and texture that will pass the ordeal of a criticism based on general observation only, you are as safe as the landscape-painter when he takes liberties with clouds and trees. But these comparisons, as to facility, between one branch of art and another, have always, or nearly always, some element of fallacy, due to the omission of some impediment. In this matter of animal-painting, people forget that although the lower animals may be easier to paint, in some respects, than men and women, they cannot be studied so conveniently. No branch of art, except what is called still-life, is so convenient to the student as the human figure. Every one who has drawn from a well-trained professional model knows the incalculable advantage of being able to correct his attitude by a word, without moving from one's place; every one who has drawn from animals has felt how grievous it is not to be able to influence their movements any more than if they were clouds or waves. There are differences, no doubt: an ox is not so lively as a dog just emerging from puppyhood; but the most staid and sober animals are the most deceptive. A pair of oxen are standing yoked to the great waggon in the farm-yard; the goad is leaning against the horn of one of them, and to any ordinary observer both the patient creatures seem as still as oxen of bronze. Now plant yourself before them with drawing materials and make a careful study; you will shortly discover that this apparent stillness conceals in reality an imperceptibly slow motion. It is the stillness of the hand on your watch, of the shadow on the sun-dial, with the difference (not in your favour) that whereas you know in what direction the hand and the shadow are going, and can make allowances accordingly, you cannot foresee the changes which the next few minutes will bring about in the outlines of a group of oxen. All waking life is naturally accompanied by continual motion, unless in the case of certain reptiles, such as the crocodile, whose death-like immobility might tempt a painter as much as its hideousness would repel him. The human model, by long practice, and an incessant effort of the will, endures one after another the thousand little uneasinesses which the mere processes of living inflict upon us; but an animal seeks relief from them in motion. The unhappy prisoners in menageries expend their irritability in movements as unceasing as they are monotonous. Even the painter's model, the dog tied on a little platform in the studio, feels the irksomeness of restraint, and has frequently to be held in position by an attendant. Some painters employ two attendants when they study animals from nature; one to hold the model, the other to occupy its attention. Is it not evident that there must always be a wide difference, in point of instructiveness, between study of this kind, so broken and interrupted, so trying to the patience, and quiet work from the living human model, who preserves his attitude whilst the student requires him, and accurately resumes it after every interval of rest? Surely in estimating the differences of facility in various departments of the fine arts we ought to take into account the opportunities for convenient study. And it may be observed, farther, that although animal form is partially concealed by fur, the concealment is much less complete than that of the human form by drapery. The truth is, that in this respect animal-painting lies half-way between that of the draped and that of the naked figure. It requires a far closer study of organization to paint the leg even of a thickly-furred animal than to paint a man's leg in a loose trowser—in the latter case it is enough to get the true creases of the cloth, and I know by careful comparison of work actually done (for this is a subject which greatly exercised my curiosity at one time) that it is *not* the best draughtsman of the nude who will give the creases best. Creases in cloth are a separate study, pushed very far, too far, at the present day, by the draughtsmen for our illustrated newspapers.

The most popular animal-painters pay close attention to the imitation of texture. This is not wrong in itself, but it is a sure sign of degradation in any art when time and care are bestowed upon the study of surface to the neglect of structure. But this is a matter which does not strictly belong to any branch of art except as a consequence of general conditions of feeling. The public mind of Europe, though greatly interested in pictures, or amused by them, was during the first twenty years of the art-revival that we have witnessed, and is still for the most part, sincerely indifferent to masterly *ordonnance* in construction, yet easily pleased by surface attraction and ornament. This spirit affected the current criticism of all the arts, but especially the criticism of poetry.

In 1853, Mr. Matthew Arnold wrote (in the Preface to the first edition of his Poems),—'We can hardly at the present day understand what Menander meant when he told a man who inquired as to the progress of his comedy that he had finished it, not having yet written a single line, because he had constructed the action of it in his mind. A modern critic would have assured him that the merit of his piece depended on the brilliant things which arose under his pen as he went along. . . . . We have critics who seem to direct their attention merely to detached expressions, to the language about the action, not to the action itself. They will permit the poet to select any action he pleases, and to suffer that action to go as it will, provided he gratifies them with occasional bursts of fine writing, and with a shower of isolated thoughts and images. That is, they permit him to leave their poetical sense ungratified, provided that he gratifies their rhetorical sense and their curiosity.'

When this preference for rhetoric over grand poetical construction exercises itself in criticism of painting it always over-estimates anything like cleverness in the imitation of texture. The temptation to do so is peculiarly strong when an animal-painter is under consideration. Every animal that painters touch is remarkable for some especial kind of surface-beauty; even the pig has a brilliant silkiness when he happens to be clean, and no fashionable artist would paint him otherwise. The soft fur of the thickly-clad bovines, the delicate fine hair of the smooth ones, the shining coats of well-groomed horses, the wavy hair of goats, the wool of sheep, the shadowy masses of mane in stallion and lion, with the rich variety of colour that they present, the russets, and yellows, and tawnies, and blacks, and delicate pale grays, and warm tones like vellum, pleasant to the eye,—all these variously beautiful textures are worth careful painting, and the very greatest artists have enjoyed them. The error of our criticism, and of our art too, is not that we enjoy these beauties of nature, which are truly amongst the purest sources of pleasure the eye can find for its refreshment ; our error is to be so enchanted with these things as to prefer the clever imitation of them to noble pictorial construction.

The right education for an animal-painter is a severe training in the figure, followed by careful drawing and dissection of dead animals. All painters do wisely to accept what science can teach them as an aid to memory, but animal-painters profit by this help even more, proportionately, than any other artists. A landscape-painter may get on without knowing the anatomy of plants, though botany would be a great help to him ; a figure-painter may surmount a difficulty by reference to the living model, but without anatomy it would be impossible to do serious work in the sculpture or design of animals. No one, who has not dissected, can know the marvel of their structure. Take, as an example, the knee of the horse (*carpus*) ; it is built up like the wall of a Highland hut, and when you think what violent shocks this little piece of God's masonry has to undergo, and when you see by actual dissection how the stones of it are fitted into their places and bound together to keep them all where they ought to be, is it not natural that after these thoughts and observations you should draw a horse's knee in action with keener interest and more accurate truth than if you thought of it merely as a rather awkward kind of hinge? And so with the wonderful pastern bones, so small and fine in the nobler races, and yet so strong and so firmly kept together by the thin tendinous prolongations of the higher muscles, that they can safely receive the whole combined weight of the horse and his rider in descending at the conclusion of a leap! Could any artist who took a hearty interest in this astonishing piece of construction ever draw it in a negligent or careless temper? All the great men who have drawn animals have recognised the importance of anatomy. How persistently Leonardo da Vinci worked at it! He, of whom it was said especially that he was *stupendissimo in far cavalli*, acquired his power by dissecting and making finished anatomical drawings, and the great equestrian statue of Francesco Sforza was prepared for with rigorous self-discipline in the accurate teachings of science. Géricault, who was one of the soundest painters of horses that ever lived, paid the same attention to anatomy.

'Géricault veut posséder *son cheval*. Il le tourne et retourne dans tous les sens. C'est une sorte de gymnastique qu'il s'impose. Il l'apprend dans ses moindres détails. Il ne néglige rien, *ni son anatomie, et sa forme intérieure*, ni les jeux de la lumière sur la robe, ni ses mouvements, si difficiles à saisir et à exprimer.'* When Landseer was examined before the Royal Academy Commission in 1863, the question was put to him whether he thought the then recently-introduced anatomical examination a change in the right direction. Sir Edwin's answer was, '*I think so: it is a very important branch of education.*'

The two things, then, which go to the production of the *animalier* are, first, the inborn, incommunicable faculty of seizing instantaneously, and long retaining, the most transient gestures of animals, with a vividness sufficient for the purposes of art; and, secondly, a scientific training in anatomy and drawing to reinforce the natural gift on all points where it may be insufficient, and give an element of accuracy and security. The first of these two possessions belonged to my obscure friend, whose humble talent may have interested the reader at the beginning of this chapter; the second, the scientific acquirement, has been attained by the laborious perseverance of many who have left no striking or admirable performance from the absence of the natural gift. Either of the two without the other is practically almost valueless. A patient and learned draughtsman

---

* *Géricault: Etude biographique et critique, par Charles Clement.*

may, no doubt, draw the body of a horse so that the muscles and bones shall be in their places in a state of perfect quiescence; but in animals the momentary attitude is the language and the life. The sculptor or painter of animals has indeed one very marked advantage over the painter of the figure—namely, this, that whereas the figure-painter is really exercising what Wordsworth contemptuously called *a dumb art*—that is, an art not capable of recording the language of the characters it represents, the art of the animal-painter is not dumb in this relative sense. A dog may bark, a horse may neigh, but it is not by these sounds that they express the delicate shades of ever-varying emotion; it is by a thousand varieties of gesture which few indeed of us can analyse, but which we easily understand. The animals are actors in a pantomime, clever beyond all human cleverness. A dog converses with his master by means of his eyes, and his ears, and his tail, nay rather by every muscle of his body. It follows from this, that whereas the figure-painter delineates a creature which (especially in modern times and in polite society) expresses little by the motions of the muscles which the painter can render, and much by words which he cannot render, the animal-painter delineates creatures whose best eloquence may be clearly expressed by his own art. The rank of animal-painting is therefore relatively higher than the rank of the creatures that it celebrates. It may be as great an achievement to paint the mind of a dog thoroughly and absolutely as to paint the mind of a man partially and imperfectly.

EE

It is scarcely necessary to add, that all artists who have delineated animals successfully have seen them with the observing clearness of affection. Emerson says that love is not a hood but an eye-water; it is so especially to artists. From what we know of men who have painted animals well in past times, it is evident that they felt towards them sentiments as far as possible removed from indifference. It is related of Da Vinci, that although several times hard-pinched for money he never could make up his mind to part with his horses, or the servants belonging to his stables, which he maintained at great expense. Horsemanship was Da Vinci's great delight, and he excelled in it. Rubens also, who painted animals grandly, rode out every day.*

Rosa Bonheur began her career by keeping a pet sheep, high up in a Parisian apartment, and in her portrait by Dubufe she leans caressingly on a fine calf which she herself introduced into the picture. Géricault had a passion for horses so strong that his biographer calls it 'une véritable frénésie.' When a fine team passed him in harness he would run by their side to watch them till he was breathless and covered with perspiration. During his college vacations he sometimes stayed with relations of his at Rouen, and there his great attraction was a blacksmith's shop, where he watched the horses from morning

---

* Géricault when a young man had for his two idols Rubens, and Franconi the circus-rider, and having remarked that the legs of Rubens were somewhat bent outwards with riding, he set himself to produce the same effect on his own by a wooden contrivance which he applied to them.

to night without intermission. He was an accomplished and most courageous rider, preferring always the most spirited horses. The same affection for the animals they draw is visible in several of our contemporaries. Bracquemont will sit for hours together watching ducks in a duck-pond; Charles Jacque, whose drawings of poultry are not the least remarkable of his works, is a great poultry-fancier. It seems needless to add that Landseer loves dogs, for he who does not must not only be incapable of painting them, but so utterly dead to all the better feelings of our nature as to be unworthy of mention in these pages.

CHAPTER XVI.

CANINE GUESTS. *

HAVING heard that two very wonderful dogs were performing within fifty miles of my house, I invited them to come and visit me. The answer came by telegraph, not from the dogs themselves, but from their owner, M. du Rouil, and on the appointed day and hour I drove off to meet them. They were invited to dine and spend the evening; and as the weather was very wet they stayed all night and breakfasted the next morning, so that I had every opportunity of making their acquaintance.

Madame du Rouil informed me that her husband had been for ten years a teacher in a deaf-and-dumb institution, which had given him the idea of trying how far a similar method of education might develope the intelligence of dogs. He had also been a conjuror, and these

---

* There is so much in this paper which must naturally seem incredible that I think it necessary to assure the reader how scrupulously I have endeavoured to narrate the facts simply as I saw them. On my honour, the narrative is, if not absolutely true, at least as true as I can make it by a comparison of what I observed myself, with the observations of a dozen other witnesses.

two professions had prepared him for the one he at present exercised. When he began to train his first dog it was not with any idea of future profit, but simply out of curiosity to see the effects of the sort of education which seemed to him best adapted for establishing a close understanding between the human and canine minds. Seeing that the plan succeeded he began to take the dog with him to the entertainments he gave in Paris, and as the public were interested he went on educating his pupil. Since then he has educated two other dogs on the same principles, one of whom has completed her training, whilst the other is an advanced, but not yet a finished, student.

I had a good opportunity, at dinner, of observing the master himself. There was not the faintest trace of anything like charlatanism in his manner. A very quiet, grave, serious, even sad-looking old gentleman, dressed soberly in black, he talked about places he had visited and about the political news of the day. The impression he made upon us was altogether favourable. He reminded me most of some respectable old school-master or librarian, who had seen a good deal of the world and reflected on what he had seen, but whose thoughts were tinged with a deepening gravity, the result of narrowed fortune and weakened health. I learned afterwards that there were ample reasons for this sadness. M. du Rouil had had two sons killed in the war and another severely wounded, whilst his daughter, a pretty girl of eighteen, had been killed by a shell at Neuilly in the sanguinary days of the Commune. His house, too, had been sacked by the Communards, and a small business which his wife managed had been put an end to. The capital invested in that little business had been earned by the dog Bianca, of whom, and her daughter Lyda, it is time to give a description.

Bianca, or Blanche, as her master familiarly calls her, is a bitch of the pure *caniche* breed. I use the French word because although we have an English one, 'poodle,' I rather think that the word poodle does not distinguish between the real *caniche* and the *chien-mouton*, another very intelligent breed from which performing dogs are frequently taken. Of M. du Rouil's three pupils one is a pure *caniche*, the other (Lyda) is a cross between the *caniche* and the spaniel, whilst the third is a *chien-mouton*, thoroughbred. The *caniche* is silky-haired and has often patches of brown about the face, but the white hair is like snow, whereas the *chien-mouton* approaches both in colour and texture much more nearly to the sheep, and never has any patches of brown. Only Blanche and Lyda came to my house; the other dog has begun to perform in public, but is not yet so accomplished as these two.

They behaved at dinner exactly like common dogs, but when I offered Blanche a piece of cheese and asked if she knew the word for that substance, her master answered that she could spell it very correctly. I had invited a few friends to meet these learned animals, and when they were assembled in the drawing-room we made the little preparations which M. du Rouil said would be most convenient. A large octagonal library-table was put in the middle of the room with a cloth of one colour and a lamp in the centre. Round this table Madame du Rouil laid cards with all the letters of the alphabet, printed in large capitals. There was also a little hand-bell. At a sign from her master Blanche jumped upon the table and sat in an attitude of expectation. Then M. du Rouil turned to me and said, 'I promised you that the dog should spell *fromage*. Blanche, spell *fromage*.' Blanche immediately set about her work and brought an F, an R, and an O, then she hesitated. 'You have only given us three letters, and there are seven in the word.' On this, she soon found M, A, G, E, and the word was complete. The next task was a translation. We were invited to write upon a slate any Latin, German, or English word in which the same letter did not occur twice. Some one present wrote, in German hand-writing, the word 𝔓𝔣𝔢𝔯𝔡, and M. du Rouil showed the slate to Blanche. She either read it or pretended to read it, and made a sign that she understood by putting the slate down with her paw. 'Now give us the French for that word;' she immediately brought C, and then H, E, V, A, L. 'As you are spending the evening at an Englishman's house, Blanche, would you oblige him by translating that word into English?' Without hesitation the dog gave me an H, and with very little hesitation the remaining letters, O, R, S, E.

Notwithstanding her success, the dog seemed to set

about her work very unwillingly, and it was evidently a great effort to her. The authority of the master, though very gently exercised, appeared to be irresistible, exactly like that of a mesmerist over his patient. Blanche complained audibly the whole time with a sound between growling and whining, and occasionally a short bark of uneasiness. Observing this, I said that for the present that part of the performance might be considered satisfactory, and we would pass on to something else. M. du Rouil then told us that Blanche could correct bad spelling, and invited me to write a word on the slate with an intentional fault in it. He showed the slate to the dog, and said, 'There is a fault here, Blanche; find it out, and show us first what letter ought to be effaced.' The word I had written was *maison*, but I had spelt it *méson*. The dog immediately brought the letter E. Then M. du Rouil requested Blanche to show us what letters ought to be substituted, and she fetched an A and an I.

As Blanche seemed tired and worried with this kind of work I intervened on her behalf, and she was allowed to go and curl herself up in a corner, and eat cakes. Lyda took her place on the table, and a set of figures were substituted for the alphabet. Some arithmetical problems were written on the state and she resolved them (or appeared to resolve them) without a single mistake. A very pretty incident occurred at this period of the performance, for the master proposed a little mental arithmetic. 'Now, Lyda,' he said, 'I want to see whether you understand division. Suppose you had ten pieces of sugar, and you met ten Prussian dogs, how many lumps would you, *une Française*, give to each of the Prussians?' Lyda very decidedly replied to this with a cipher. 'But now suppose that you divided your lumps of sugar with me, how many would you give me?' Lyda took up the figure 5, and presented it to her master.

This was pretty enough, but for reasons of my own I was much more interested in something that happened immediately afterwards. M. du Rouil *quitted the room*, the door was closed after him, and he called out, 'Which is the least valuable figure?' Lyda brought me the cipher. Then her master said, 'Which is the most valuable figure?' the dog brought me the 9. After this I asked for different figures, which the dog gave me without a single mistake.

It was Blanche's turn next, but this time instead of being surrounded with the letters of the alphabet she was surrounded with playing-cards. M. du Rouil had another pack in his hand, and told us to choose a card. 'Blanche, what card has been chosen?' The dog always took up the right card in her teeth. Then she played a game with a young lady, and lost it, after which she rushed from her seat into the corner with an air of the deepest humiliation.

A very surprising thing followed the game at cards. M. du Rouil begged me to go into another room and leave a light on the floor with a pack of cards arranged all round it and to close the doors as nearly as possible without shutting them. This being done, he begged any one present to whisper in the dog's ear the name of a card to be fetched by her from the other room. A lady whispered the 'knave of hearts,' if I remember rightly, but in so low a voice as to be inaudible even by the dog, which made a mistake, and brought something else. She was then requested to bring the ace of spades, and she soon came back from the dining-room with the ace of spades in her teeth.

Both the dogs played a game at dominoes. This was managed as follows: the dogs sat on chairs opposite each other, and took up the domino that was wanted; but the master or mistress placed it, and kept announcing the state of the game. Their distress when they could not go on without drawing upon the bank was expressed in piteous whines, and amused us all immensely. Lyda was the loser, and she precipitately retreated to hide herself, with an evident consciousness of defeat.

I had not quite done with my literary examination of Bianca, so I had the alphabet replaced and began again. I asked her what was the English for *chien*, and she put the letters D, O, G, into my own hand. Then I asked her to spell *feu* for me, and she gave me the three letters F, E, U. Here an incident occurred which, notwithstanding the marvels we had witnessed, thrilled us all with new amazement. M. du Rouil interposed, and said, very gently, ' Blanche, you have spelt the word correctly in the singular, but cannot you give the plural?' My readers may believe me or not, as they like, but the truth is, that she took up the letter X between her teeth and came to me and placed it in my hand. I asked her to give me the English for *feu*, and wrote it down and handed it to M. du Rouil, but he said she had not yet learned that word, and this defect in her education could not be remedied at once.

During the whole of this entertainment my mind was intently occupied with a single problem, *What did the dogs really know?* I had been told a few days previously, by a gentleman who had very keen powers of observation, that a system of signals existed between M. du Rouil and his dogs, by which he made them understand which card they ought to take, and this gentleman believed that he had detected the most important signal of all. 'When M. du Rouil means *no* he advances towards the table, and when he means *yes* he retires from it.' Another observer, younger and much less intelligent, had told me that M. du Rouil, having been a teacher of the deaf and dumb, simply used signs with his fingers, which the dogs had learned to read. These two theories may be disposed of very summarily. When the entertainment began with the literary examination of Bianca, M. du Rouil stood on the hearth-rug, with his back to the fire, and did not advance or retreat one inch; whilst at the conclusion, when she gave the plural to the word *feu*, I myself occupied M. du Rouil's place, and he was seated in an arm-chair, like the other spectators, and with his back to the table. It is clear, therefore, that the theory about advancing and retreating is not an explanation. Now, as for the other theory, that he communicates with the dogs by means of manual signs, like those used with the deaf and dumb, I need only observe that M. du Rouil's hands were as motionless as his feet. When we began with *fromage, pferd*, &c., he held a tray in his right hand, the arm being pendent by his side, whilst the left hand was behind his back, the fingers closed, and as motionless as those of a bronze Napoleon on a chimney-piece. He did not even reserve to himself such liberty of motion as might have been secured by taking the letters from the dog, for when I proposed to take the letters myself he made no objection whatever, but sat down quietly and let me do the showman's work. It is certain that the communication was not made by any motion of the body; this, at least, I can affirm quite positively. Was it done by the expression of the eyes? At first we thought that this might be just possible; but the table was octagonal, and the dog found the letters when her back was turned to her master as easily as when she could look him in the face; besides, when M. du Rouil was seated, and I was the showman, he did not look towards the dog at all, but at the fire. Whatever communication did take place must have been entirely by intonations of the voice, but we could hear these as well as the dogs could, and with all our listening we could detect nothing like a regularly recurring and easily recognisable signal. When he asked Blanche to turn *feu* into the plural, he did it exactly with the words and in the manner that you would use to a child at school. He often encouraged the dogs with such words as *Allons, allons! Cherchez, cherchez bien! Vite, vite, vite!* but he went on with these encouragements exactly in the same words and in the same tone after the word was completed to put the dog's knowledge to the test, and she went on seeking, and then whined and rang a bell to say that there were no more letters needed. I had been told that Blanche could, of course, spell any word that her master could spell, because she only took the letters he fixed upon, yet he said she could not spell *fire* for me. This, however, may have been a ruse on his part, and I do not insist upon it.

If the dogs had appeared to know rather less we should have believed that the knowledge was really theirs, but then they seemed to know too much. Lyda showed us some tricks with numbers, that are familiar to arithmeticians, but clearly beyond the canine comprehension. This satisfied me that some communication existed, and yet I was utterly unable to detect it. It is clear, therefore, that the dogs understood and acted upon a system of signalling which the intelligence of the human spectators was not keen enough to discover. I had invited several intelligent friends, and told them previously that my object was to discover the secret of the confederacy between M. du Rouil and his dogs, begging their best assistance. They watched him as closely as I did, but could detect nothing.

Remembering an odd notion of Sydney Smith's, that people might be taught to read by odours, the idea occurred to me that M. du Rouil might contrive to touch the cards that the dogs selected, and curiously enough they certainly smelt them rather than looked at them. But how could such a supposition be reconcilable with the fact that M. du Rouil kept at a distance from the table, and could not possibly foresee the words that we asked for? I only mention this hypothesis of reading by odour to show to what straits we were reduced in our guessing.

As the dogs and their owner were to stay all night at my house, I determined to have a quiet talk with him when everybody else was gone, and get at the secret if I could. So when we were quite alone together I plied him with indiscreet questions, and he was frank enough up to a certain point, but beyond that point absolutely impenetrable.

He confessed at once that there was a secret, but he said, '*La ficelle est bien cachée,*' as indeed it was. According to his account, which was probably quite true as far as it went, the dogs were like actors, who had not quite thoroughly mastered their parts, and he himself was like the prompter near the footlights. To begin with, Blanche really knew the letters of the alphabet and the playing-cards by their names, and Lyda really knew all the figures. In addition to this, he said that Blanche had studied about a hundred and fifty words in different languages, something like twenty in each language, words most likely to be called for, such as *chien*, dog, horse, cat, pferd, canis, &c., &c. The restriction to one set of letters simplified the business considerably. But M. du Rouil confessed quite frankly that she could not get through a word unless he were present. On the other hand, he could not make her spell a word in public that she had not before practised with him in private. So it was with Lyda and the figures. She really knew the figures when isolated, and this had been satisfactorily demonstrated when he left the room, and she gave me the number asked for, up to 9. But he would not tell me the secret of the confederacy. I told him what guesses had been made on the subject, but he simply answered that I must have observed how impossible it was for him to make signs with hands or feet when he moved neither hand nor foot.

Would he give me some account of the earlier stages of training through which these dogs had passed? Yes, very willingly. The first thing was to teach a dog to fetch an object, the next to make him discriminate between one of two very different objects placed together, and bring one or the other as it was mentioned by its name. In beginning the alphabet he put two most dissimilar letters side by side to begin with, such as an O and an I, avoiding the confusion of similar ones, such as O and Q, or B and R. Gradually, the dog became observant enough to discriminate between letters in which the difference was not so marked. M. du Rouil told me that he had found the greatest difficulty in teaching

Blanche to distinguish between the knaves and kings in playing-cards, but that she learned the aces very promptly. With regard to the time required for educating a dog sufficiently to perform in public, he said that an hour a day for eighteen months was the time required, and he preferred a single hour to a longer lesson, because the dog's powers of attention were soon fatigued. He added, that it was impossible to educate a dog at any other time than the middle of the night, because the slightest sound disturbed it, and made it forget the work that had to be done. I inquired what, after his ten years' experience, was his opinion of the intelligence of dogs, and he answered, with great emphasis, 'that it is. infinite.'

Beyond this he would tell nothing. The only supposition not immediately annihilated by the facts, is that the *tone of voice* used in uttering the words '*Allons, allons; Cherchez, cherchez bien; Cherchez encore; Vite, vite, vite,*' conveyed to the animal, 'You are far from the card,' 'You are nearer the card,' 'That is the card you must take up;' but even here there were great difficulties, for M. du Rouil continued, as far as we could detect, in the same tone after the completion of the word, and yet the dog never brought a superfluous letter. The marvellousness of so perfect a confederacy may be better understood by supposing a human confederate in the dog's place. Such a human confederate, not knowing the words to be composed, would be very liable to make mistakes, and bring a wrong letter from time to time;

but Blanche never made one mistake—never brought one wrong letter.

I certainly observed that when she got near the letter she always hesitated between it and its neighbours on each side, but she always finally took the letter that was wanted. She got on much faster with one or two words than she did with the others, and seemed to need less encouragement. My conclusion was, that from long practice with certain familiar words (she had worked at the business daily for several years) she could compose those words with very little help. The last word, *feu*, and the X to make a plural of it, were given quickly, others not so quickly. The use of the X was clever, but not so surprising as it seemed to us at the moment, for with a dog so well trained as Blanche it would be easy, I should imagine, to associate the word 'plural' with the image of the letter X. Very probably Blanche had been taught, in her private lessons, to fetch that letter whenever '*pluriel*' was asked for. As for the translation, without going so far in credulity as to fancy that the dog really translated, I may suggest that from long practice there would certainly arise in her mind an association of ideas between *cheval* and *horse*, *chien* and *dog*, since the words must have been asked for hundreds or thousands of times in that close connection, so that she would at least be better prepared to spell *dog*, after having just spelt *chien*.

An incident occurred in the course of the evening which showed some understanding of language. A little girl wanted Blanche to come to her, but the dog kept away, on which Madame du Rouil said, 'Blanche, allez saluer la petite demoiselle.' She immediately went up to the little girl and made a formal obeisance. A lady present, the daughter of a landowner in the Sologne, told us that on her father's estate the shepherds' dogs were taught to go in four directions at the word of command —*à droite, à gauche, en avant,* and *en arrière.*

The conclusion we arrived at was, that the performance resulted from an extremely clever combination of previous training with scarcely perceptible prompting, that the dogs were really wonderfully educated and knew a great deal, though not so much as they appeared to know. The game at dominoes was decidedly the prettiest instance of their real knowledge, for they took up the numbers just as they were asked for. It seems evident that an intelligent dog might be taught to know a considerable variety of objects by their names.

M. du Rouil told us an anecdote of Blanche which may be easily believed by any one who has made her acquaintance. He was going home one night from Paris to Neuilly, after a performance, and saw a man who was seeking for some object that he had lost. 'What are you seeking?' he asked. The man answered that he had lost 280 francs. 'Possibly my dog may be able to find them for you; have you any money left? If you have, show her a piece of gold. *Allez, cherchez, Blanche!*' The dog set out and fetched first one piece of gold and then another and then a bank-note till the 280 francs were completed. Then followed many other anecdotes about dogs of which I select these. A lady said that she had known a dog that belonged to a celebrated publisher in Paris who had a country-house at Auteuil. Every Friday his family went to Auteuil, and always regularly found the dog there on their arrival. He went alone, through Paris, from the *Rue de l'Ancienne Comédie*, and he never made a mistake about the day. The family frequently went out on other days, but on these occasions the dog stayed contentedly at home. Another dog that she had also known had been bred in a strictly Catholic family, and would never touch meat on a Friday. Bets were made, and the greatest temptations used to overcome his conscientious scruples, but always in vain. He was shut up in a room during a whole Friday with meat in his reach, but preferred to suffer hunger rather than touch it. One of my friends mentioned a dog that he knew quite well which lost its master three years ago from small-pox, and ever since then, in all weathers, has paid a daily visit to the cemetery, where it mourns upon his grave. The widow goes to the grave on Sundays after mass, the dog knows this, waits for her at the church-door, and accompanies her.

Lyda has one quality which would make her invaluable to an artist. Every painter who has attempted to draw dogs knows how provokingly restless they always are, and how impossible it is to study them as we do the human model. But Lyda *poses* as perfectly as any human model at the Royal Academy. I made a drawing of her the morning after the performance and was delighted. *Literally not a hair stirred during the whole time.* She had the stillness of a stuffed animal in a museum, with that perfection of living form which no taxidermist was ever yet able to imitate or preserve. A dog so perfectly trained as Lyda would be a priceless treasure for an animal-painter. Blanche *poses* fairly well, but she is not to be compared with Lyda. I wish I could give some notion of Lyda's eyes; they have the strangest half-human expression, as if there were half a soul behind them. Her master says that she looks at him with an intensity that is quite painful when she is trying with all her might to understand what he wishes her to learn. I declare that this creature's looks are enough to frighten you if you dwell upon them, it seems as if some unhappy child-soul had been imprisoned in that canine shape. Are these poor dogs happy in their strange, unnatural life? They are tenderly cared for, and their master says that whoever beats a dog gives evidence of his own personal stupidity, for a dog always tries his best to understand, and you can make things clearest to him by gentle teaching if you know how to teach at all. And still these dogs look over-wrought, and nervously anxious, they have just the very look which you may notice in over-worked professional men. Ah, poor humble canine brethren, specimens of mental culture, are we not in the same perilous trade? And would it not have been better for all three of us if instead of giving ourselves up to letters we had passed a careless, sylvan life under the good green wood? *

* M. du Rouil died a few days after his visit to my house, and his widow immediately sold or gave away the three dogs; a clear proof of the truth of her assertion that she did not know how her husband managed them, or at least that if his method were theoretically known to her she was unable to put it into practice. The present owners of these animals can get no performance out of them whatever. I have now no hope of ascertaining the true secret of M. du Rouil's confederacy with his dogs; but the mere fact that so perfect a confederacy should exist proves the keenest intelligence on their part. Whatever may have been the signals used they were understood without error by the dogs, and yet the human observers, although using their human faculties at the full stretch of excited curiosity, were utterly unable to detect them.

www.ingramcontent.com/pod-product-compliance
Lightning Source LLC
Chambersburg PA
CBHW021349230426
43666CB00006B/455